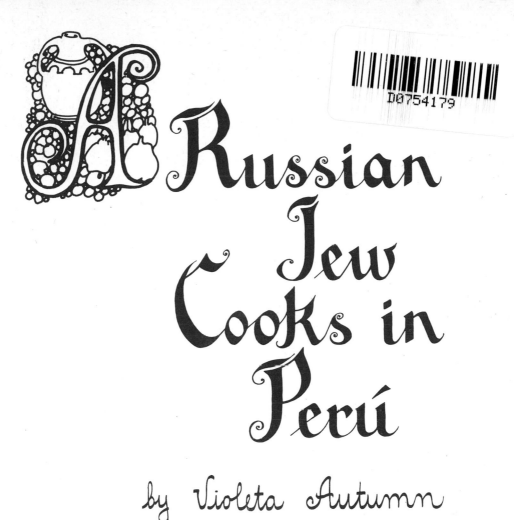

A Russian Jew Cooks in Perú

by Violeta Autumn

Design, illustrations and calligraphy by the author

101 Productions   San Francisco   1973

Second Printing, October, 1974

Copyright © 1973 Violeta Autumn

Printed in the United States of America
All Rights Reserved

Distributed to the Book Trade in the United States of America
by Charles Scribner's Sons, New York

Distributed in Canada
by Van Nostrand Reinhold Ltd., Scarborough, Ontario

Library of Congress Catalog Card Number 73-81086

PUBLISHED BY 101 PRODUCTIONS
834 Mission Street
San Francisco, California 94103

Contents

To the memory of my Mother
who fortunately permitted
small kibitzers in her kitchen

Preface

In the late 20's and early 30's there was an influx of Russian-born Jewish people to Peru. They were young people from the small towns lining the frontiers of Russia and Roumania, along the river Prut in the region of Bessarabia. These young people all had their reason for leaving, be it the hard times in the old country after World War I, the stories of unbelievable opportunities as told by the adventurers that preceded them to the New World or their own sense of adventure.

Anyhow, they left Russia and they found themselves in Peru. Short of the differences in physical appearance, language and social customs, the immigrants found that things had not really changed; they found themselves in towns just as small as the ones they had left and in the company of people just as poor as they were.

The stories told of these arrivals, of their disappointments, befuddlement and despair would be sad if they were not filled with that irrepressible sense of humor and good-natured tolerance so characteristic of their group. It wasn't long before the shock of arrival wore off and they were speaking Spanish, eating seviche and dancing the marinera with just as much gusto as their genial and accepting hosts.

Basically, immigrants as a breed only last one generation; they create a chance condition that is fragile in its permanence. The immigrant never loses his traditional ways, but he does assimilate the new, and so manages to create something unique which lives as he lives and then it's gone.

And that is what this book is all about. It is an attempt at recording one such moment in history that happens to taste awfully good.

Any similarity to
Kosher cookery is
purely coincidental.

ABBREVIATIONS & CONVERSION TABLES

lb... pounds
oz... ounces
Qt... quarts
pt... pints
c... cups
T... tablespoons
t... teaspoons
hr... hours
min.. minutes
H_2O.. water

½"... one half inch
1"... one inch

S ... salt

P ... pepper

300°F ... oven temperature in degrees Fahrenheit

oil .. cooking & salad oil, like safflower or corn oil.

EQUIVALENTS

1	lb. flour	4	c	±
1	lb. sugar	2	c	
1	lb. butter	2	c	
1	lb. powdered sugar	2 ⅔	c	
1	pt. liquid	2	c	
1	Qt.	2	pt.	
1	c	16	T	
1	T	3	t	

7

Russky Snacks

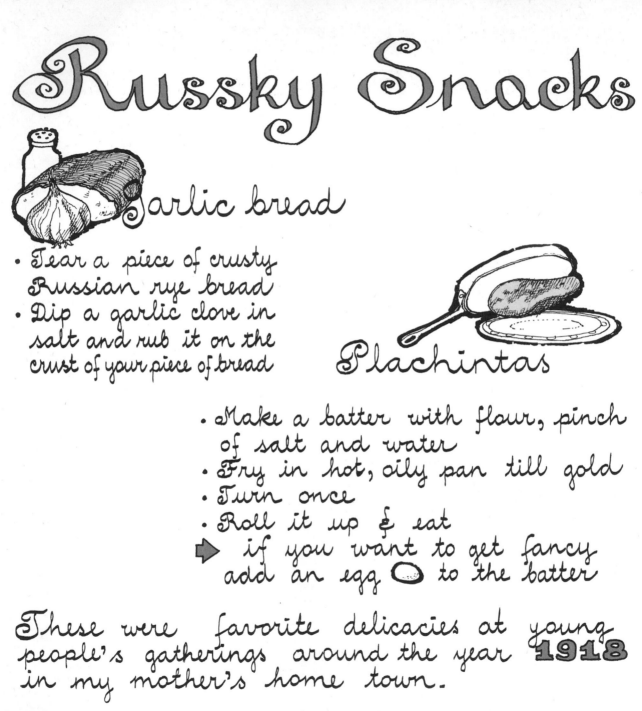

Garlic bread

- Tear a piece of crusty Russian rye bread
- Dip a garlic clove in salt and rub it on the crust of your piece of bread

Plachintas

- Make a batter with flour, pinch of salt and water
- Fry in hot, oily pan till gold
- Turn once
- Roll it up & eat
  ➡ if you want to get fancy add an egg ⬭ to the batter

These were favorite delicacies at young people's gatherings around the year **1918** in my mother's home town.

Onion & Matzo

- Dip a piece of onion in shmaltz
- Rub on a piece of matzo & sprinkle with salt

Tea

Tea leaves in strainer ➡

Heat glass before pouring ➡

Hanky handle ➡

Sugar cubes (must be held between front teeth) ➡

boiling water ➡

kettle or samovar

Always serve Hot tea ⬆

and

⬅ lemon

with snacks.

9

Dill Pickles
no vinegar

This recipe will yield about 6 quarts of pickles

Stir ¼ c rock salt in 1 c boiling water until thoroughly dissolved

Add 4 c cold water

Wash 6 lb. pickling cucumbers in cold water until they sparkle

1 sprig fresh flower dill

1 whole hot pepper

1 garlic clove

1 t pickling spice

spices in each quart

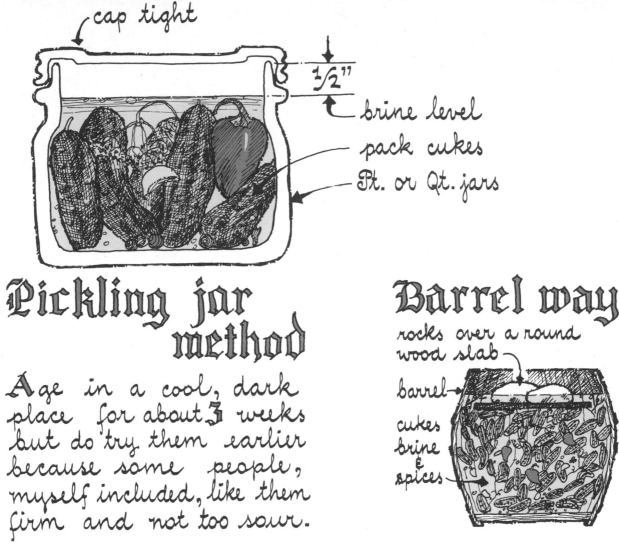

cap tight

1/2"

brine level
pack cukes
Pt. or Qt. jars

Pickling jar method

Age in a cool, dark place for about 3 weeks but do try them earlier because some people, myself included, like them firm and not too sour.

Barrel way

rocks over a round wood slab

barrel

cukes
brine
&
spices

The brine, when the pickles are done is called ROSS'L and may be served, strained, in small jiggers to be sipped during dinner.

JREIN

Beet horseradish relish

1 grate fresh peeled horseradish root

OR

1 soak each 4 T dry horseradish in 1½ c hot water until soft ➡ let cool

2 Cook bunch fresh beets ➡ cool ➡ peel ➡ grind

3 Mix: 1½ c + 2 c + 3 T + 2 T + S
grated horseradish   ground beets   white vinegar   sugar   1/4 t

4 Taste and adjust if you must

5 Refrigerate in closed containers

Jrein is traditionally served with gefilte fish but we used it with almost anything.

INSTANT JREIN

commercial horseradish	drained canned beets. ground up	white vinegar	⅛ t S
¼ c PREPARED	16 oz.	1 T	1 T SUGAR

1 HR. pickled peppers

2 red sweet peppers

red wine vinegar

2 garlic cloves

a Singe peppers on direct flame until they are black all over.
b Peel & take out seeds and veins, slice and place in a bowl.

garlic cloves cut in 4
vinegar to cover
sliced peppers

Marinate **1 HR.**
chill and serve with dinner

Avocado a la Brasilera

2 medium, ripe avocados
(the oilier & yellower the better)

2 t lemon juice

1 t

¼ t

➡️ **Mash the Works & Chill** ⬅️

Serve in small chilled bowls
surrounded by cucumber slices
as an appetizer or salad or as
a dip for toasted strips of bread
or melba toast.

Chopped Liver

A. ½ lb. beef liver - broiled or fried

B. Remove ducts and grind till very smooth

cleaver   or grinder   or   blender   or   mouli

C. Add: 2 T shmaltz or margarine
   1 hard-boiled egg chopped very fine
   1 small chopped onion
   ⅛ t pepper but ➡ hold the salt ⬅

D. Refrigerate covered with wax paper

E. Add salt at time of serving ⬅

Never store chopped liver after
it has been salted because it
turns onions black and watery
and bitter.

Variation: Omit egg and onion, add extra T
margarine and go ahead and add the salt.

Chopped Egg

3 eggs Hard-boiled - chopped fine

1 T shmaltz or margarine   S & P

2 T onion - chopped fine

Mix it all up & serve on lettuce leaf & garnish with a sprig of parsley.

Chopped Eggplant

Large eggplant.

medium torpedo onion   chopped fine

1 T vinegar or lemon juice

1 T salad oil   S & P

chopped piece tomato & green pepper (Optional)

Broil eggplant until all skin black and eggplant looks quite limp ➡ Let cool ➡ Peel ➡ Mash Add other ingredients ➡ Mash, taste & fuss with it till ➡ Just Right ⬅

Serve on lettuce leaf & garnish with sliced tomatoes and turnips.

17

Pickled Herring

1 **2** cleaned salted herrings ➤ soak a few hours in cold water ➤ change water twice

2 Cut in pieces · discard both ends

3 Slice **2** white onions in rings

4 Make the solution ➤

1 C   white vinegar
       bay leaves
ΥΥΥ   cloves (optional)
½ t   sugar
⅛ t   peppercorns
       (the big red ones)

Bring to a boil & Cool

5 Pack

tighten
cap

solution
to cover

onions

fish

onions

fish

onions

fish

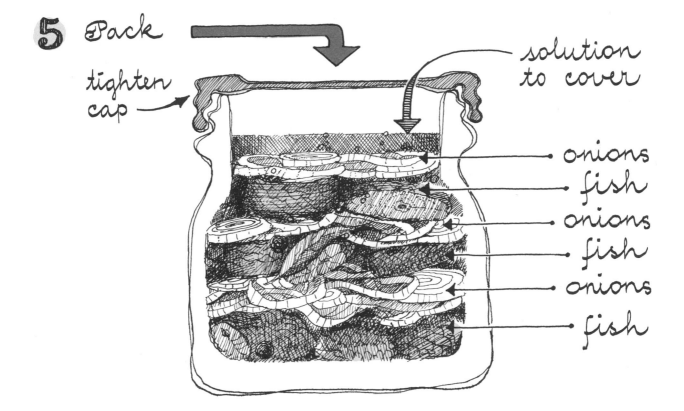

6 Refrigerate ➤ It should be ready in **2** to **3** days

JUMUS

The first time I tried jumus was in an Arab restaurant in Israel. We had been walking all day and had developed ravenous appetites; so when we saw that our fare consisted of a thin coating at the bottom of our plate, all we could think of was "Is that all we get?" One taste was enough to justify the dish. Jumus has become very popular in Perú where it is served as an appetizer or party dip.

1 C drained cooked or canned garbanzos

blender

2 T tahini (crushed sesame seeds)
Juice of 1 lemon (or more)
dash garlic salt
S & P
small piece hot pepper (optional)

Blend to a smooth paste.

bit olive oil on top — sprinkle paprika & parsley
Individual small flat plate — thin layer Jumus

Serve unleavened bread and no silverware.

Black bean Soup

- Soak **1** c washed black beans in 4 c water **1** hr.
- In the meantime make a broth ➡
  - **1** lb. marrow bones
  - 4 c cold water
- Bring to boil ➡ lower heat ➡ simmer **1**½ hrs.
  cool broth ➡ skim fat ➡ then add:

broth +
beans + water
= 8 c

- the beans in their water
- **1** sliced carrot
- 2 T barley
- **1** T dried mushrooms
- **1** t fresh hot pepper-no seeds

- simmer until beans and barley are tender
- Add the *Ambren* (Yiddish touch) ➡ stir & serve.

1 T oil, 2 t flour

stirring fry till golden

serves 8

PESTO

In a mortar & pestle
➡ Mash: { **1** garlic clove
S & P
1/2 t sweet basil (fresh if available)

➡ Add & keep { 2 T goat's cheese or Parmesan
mashing { 3 T cooking oil

This amount of pesto will flavor a menestrón for 6 or 8

Menestrón

In a large pot brown ➡ 🧅 **1** large chopped onion in **2 T** shmaltz or oil

 Add :

 beef broth ➡ just enough to float the goodies

 piece of purple cabbage

some green beans

Optional ➡ tomato 🍅

and some green peas

 couple stalks of celery

a piece of pumpkin or banana squash

1 potato

1 carrot and a handful of rice

➡ Cut the vegetables in healthy pieces, do not mince

➡ simmer uncovered till vegetables done but not mushy

⬅———— Go make the pesto

➡ Pour a ⬛C of liquid from the soup into the mortar

➡ Pour the contents of the mortar into the soup

➡ Let pot rest a bit out of the fire ➡ then serve.

Menestrón is not a precise soup, variations are O.k.

Barley~Lima bean Soup

Make a broth

2 celery stalks-leaves too
6 c cold water
1 whole onion

2 lb. soup bones

Bring to boil ➡ lower heat ➡ simmer ⬛ 1½ hrs.
Cool broth ➡ skim fat ➡ strain ➡ then add:

barley   lima beans

½ c   ½ c   S   P

2 carrots

sprig parsley

¼ t sweet basil

Broth + water = 8 c

Simmer until barley is tender, about ⬛ 1½ hrs.
Option ➡ if there is meat on the bones cut in
small pieces & add to soup.   serves 8

Latin Lentil Soup

• Soak  **1** c washed lentils in **4** c water **1** hr.

In the meantime fry:

crushed garlic clove

chopped onion ➤

cut up tomato - no skin no seeds

2 T oil

piece salt pork

• When all is nice and saucy add the lentils in their water, **1** sliced carrot and **4** c water ✳

• Bring to a boil ➤ lower heat ➤ simmer about 1½ hrs. stirring occasionally.

• When lentils are tender add ⑤ & ⑥ to taste ➤ Serve.

• Cut the tip of a hot pepper and let whoever dares dip it once, or twice into their bowl of soup (make sure no one forgets to take it out).

✳ Peruvians eat their soup, not drink it, if you prefer to drink yours add more water.   serves **8**

Borsht with Meat

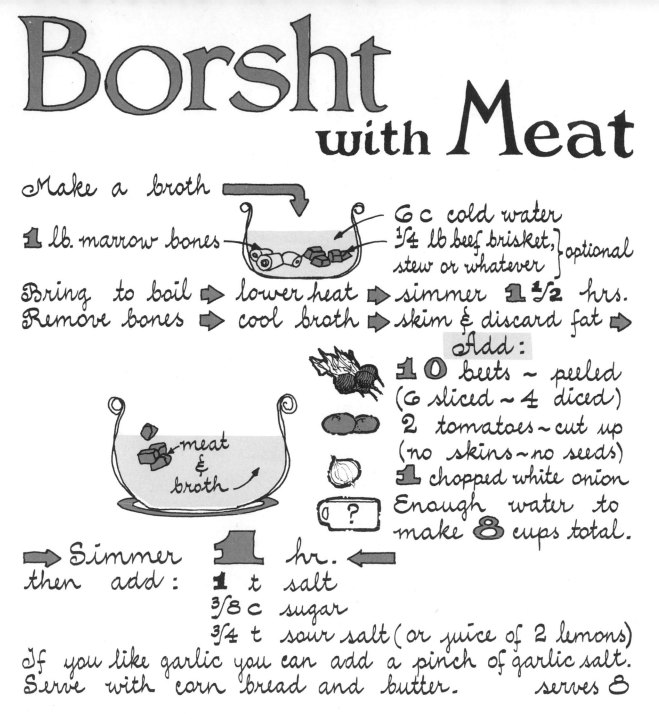

Make a broth

1 lb. marrow bones — 6 c cold water
¼ lb beef brisket, stew or whatever } optional

Bring to boil ➡ lower heat ➡ simmer 1½ hrs.
Remove bones ➡ cool broth ➡ skim & discard fat ➡

Add :

10 beets ~ peeled
(6 sliced ~ 4 diced)
2 tomatoes ~ cut up
(no skins ~ no seeds)
1 chopped white onion
Enough water to make 8 cups total.

meat & broth

➡ Simmer 1 hr. ⬅
then add : 1 t salt
3/8 c sugar
3/4 t sour salt (or juice of 2 lemons)
If you like garlic you can add a pinch of garlic salt.
Serve with corn bread and butter.   serves 8

26

cold Borsht with sour cream

6 beets ➡ peel ➡ grate & boil in 6 c water ➡ Simmer 30 min.

Add ➡ 3/4 t salt ➡ 1/4 c sugar ➡ 1/2 t sour salt ➡ test for taste ➡ strain & chill

To 1/2 pt sour cream add slowly the chilled borsht mixing as you go.

The color is nice, so capitalize ➡ Serve it in chilled clear glass bowls. ➡ In the U.S. the sour cream is not mixed with the borsht but is served as a white floating island on a red sea, which might sound a bit more Russian.

pseudo Borsht

can beets + can cream vegetable soup + water as called for in soup can } Bring to a boil

Add ➡ 1/8 t sour salt & 3 T sugar ➡ chill & serve.

CHUPE

chowder

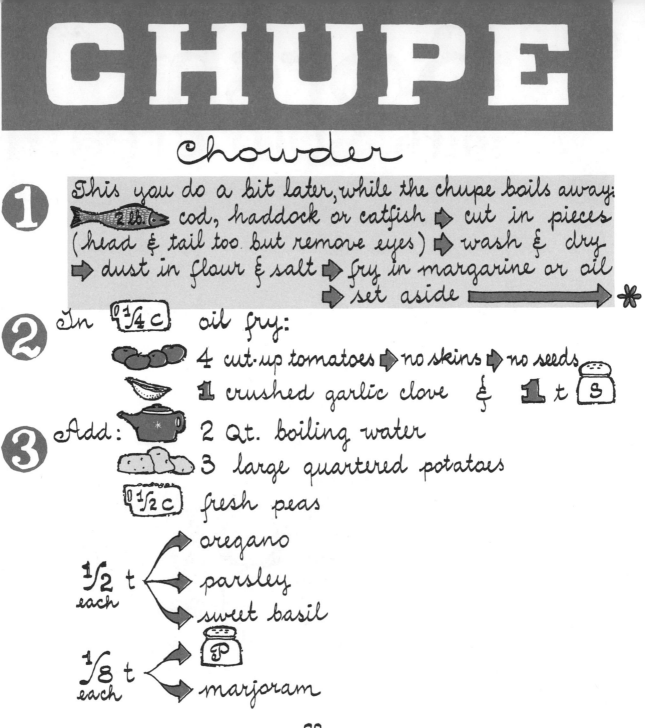

1 This you do a bit later, while the chupe boils away: 2 lb. cod, haddock or catfish ➤ cut in pieces (head & tail too but remove eyes) ➤ wash & dry ➤ dust in flour & salt ➤ fry in margarine or oil ➤ set aside ⟶ *

2 In ¼ c oil fry:

4 cut-up tomatoes ➤ no skins ➤ no seeds

1 crushed garlic clove & 1 t S

3 Add: 2 Qt. boiling water

3 large quartered potatoes

½ c fresh peas

½ t each ➤ oregano
➤ parsley
➤ sweet basil

⅛ t each ➤ P
➤ marjoram

4 Bring to a boil ➡ lower heat ➡ simmer until potatoes are cooked but firm ➡ then add:

1 Qt. boiling milk

1 lb. peeled & deveined shrimps

➡ Taste for salt & Test for thickness ⬅

➡ If soup is too thick add hot water ➡ if too thin mash a couple of the pieces of potato.

5 In 2 or 3 min. when shrimps are done take pot off fire and add forthwith:

2 eggs beaten with

⑤ 1/8 t and

small piece hot pepper ➡ no seeds

*6 Now you add the fried fish and let the pot rest for **5** min. ➡ then serve.

offer lemon.   serves 10 to 12

CHILCANO

This is a dish native to the town of Chilca near Lima, and is much appreciated by the Criollos especially after a night of excessive drinking of spirits.

2 lb. sea bass, mackerel or other coarse fleshed oily fish, head & tail too but remove eyes

3 green onions
save the heads
cook the tails

boiling water 3 C

1 Lower heat & simmer for **5** min. only

2 Remove from fire

3 Add ➡ to the whole pot or to individual portions :

lemon juice to taste
minced green onion heads
bit crushed hot pepper

CAUTION ➡

serves 4

Serve immediately with French bread and butter and call it lunch or dinner, as the case may be.

Escabeche
Fish vinaigrette

2 lb. fresh bass, butterfish, sole or other fish in season

1 fillet or cut in pieces; and in cooking oil:

2 fry lightly ➡ then set aside ➡

3 cut 🧅🧅 3 onions in thin strips

4 cook onions in $\frac{1}{4}$c wine vinegar

5 when vinegar has evaporated add $\frac{1}{4}$c oil and 🌶 cut-up hot pepper & fry till golden.

6 In skillet arrange thus:

2 T H_2O

fried onions and hot pepper

fried fish

7 cook till water is absorbed
➡ Let cool ⬅

8 serve ornamented with black olives and hard-boiled eggs.   serves 4

Seviche

(a raw fish dish)

Seviche is a typically "Criollo" dish. Criollo refers to South Americans who trace their ancestry to Europe, but by now Criollo is used, with a slight tinge of pride, to describe the Peruano especially along the coastal region

In Perú seviche is traditionally made with corvina, a superb local fish. In the States I have made a pretty authentic seviche using sea bass, halibut and other firm white fish.

Seviche is served at the beginning of the meal with cold boiled sweet potatoes, corn on the cob and yucca roots.

In the Northern Hemisphere yucca grows in Mexico, some parts of the Middle West and in Fresno, California and is distributed to other parts of the United States around Easter time.

Cut in **1**" cubes
no skin, no bones

lemon juice to
cover fish cubes

Bowl # **1**

2 onions in rings
washed in very salted
water then rinsed

juice of another lemon

2 hot peppers in
rings (include seeds
only if you are reckless)

Bowl # **2**

In **5** min. dump contents of bowl # **2**
on contents of bowl # **1** and let it
marinate for **1** hour or **2**.

Dish out carefully so you don't mix it
all up.
Will serve 4 to 8 depending on what else is for dinner.

Shrimp Seviche

1 lb. shrimps ➡ peel ➡ devein ➡ wash & cook in boiling water 1 min. drain and let them cool

1 large onion ➡ cut in rings ➡ wash in very salty water ➡ rinse & drain

1 hot pepper ➡ cut in long strips ➡ seeds out

S P ➡ to taste

Place the works in a deep bowl and cover with the juice of **4** to **5** lemons

Let rest **2** hours

Refrigerate covered until serving time. Serve with cold boiled sweet potatoes and yucca roots (see p. 32) or corn on the cob.

☞ You will please note that contrary to the directions for fish seviche you are allowed to mix it all up.

Gefilte Fish

2 lb. fish ➡ white, sea bass, halibut, pike, dore or other mild tasting fish. { skin & debone

1 T raw onion

1 t salt

½ t pepper

2 eggs

1 T fried onion with **1** T of the oil (see p. 40)

1 t sugar in **1** T water

5 T matzo meal ⬅ approximately ➡ enough to make a mixture that can be shaped

A chop fish and onion to a smooth mass

B add all other ingredients

C with wet hands shape so: ➡ ⟵ 3" ⟶ ⬅ patty

D drop patties gently into

1 T fried onion & **1** T of the oil (see p. 40) ➡ boiling 4 c water ⬅ **1** t salt ¼ t pepper

E Reduce heat & simmer 20 min. ➡ add sliced raw potato & simmer 20 min. more ➡ chill ➡ serves 4 to 6

Gefilte fish, meaning literally stuffed fish, got its name from the way it was originally made, in Roumania I think. The flesh and bones used to be removed very carefully so as to leave the skin pretty well intact. The stuffing was then prepared and put back into the skin which was subsequently sewed up to look as close to the fish's original self as possible. We don't do that in this recipe.

OKOPA

Okopa is an Indian dish originally made by mashing to a pulp toasted corn flour, dried vegetables, dried river shrimp, roasted peanuts, hot peppers and water. This makes a heavy sauce which is eaten over potatoes or other starchy vegetables.

Okopa constitutes one of the main meals during trips or in the fields, since most ingredients are carried dry.

OKOPA AREQUIPEÑA

This is one modern version as prepared in Arequipa, the white city at the foot of the volcano Misti.

Blend as you add in order ➡ till smooth ⬅

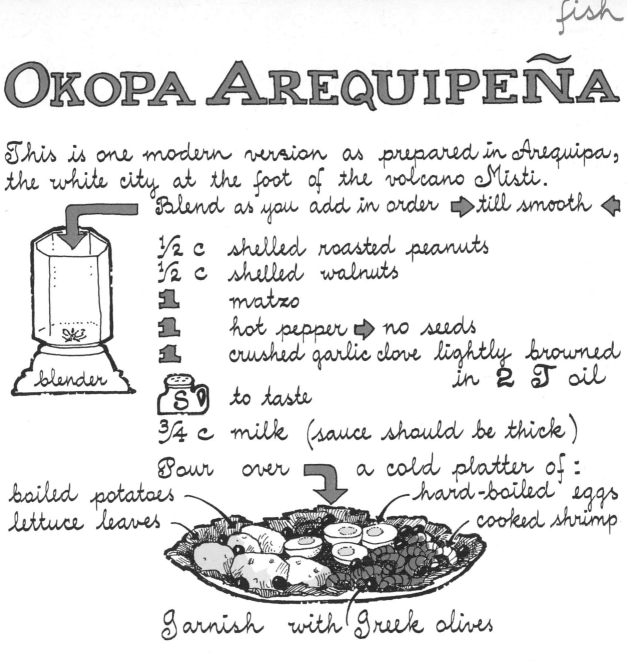

blender

½ c	shelled roasted peanuts
½ c	shelled walnuts
1	matzo
1	hot pepper ➡ no seeds
1	crushed garlic clove lightly browned in **2** T oil
S	to taste
¾ c	milk (sauce should be thick)

Pour over ➡ a cold platter of:

boiled potatoes — hard-boiled eggs
lettuce leaves — cooked shrimp

Garnish with Greek olives

This amount of sauce will cover a platter for 4 to 6.

Fried Onions for Cooking

This is the secret of what makes Yiddish dishes taste so Yiddish and also what makes Peruvian dishes taste Yiddish too. Potato varenikes, essek fleish and varnishkes would never be the same without it. It is time consuming, to be sure, but if you make a whole bunch and store capped in your refrigerator for future use it's not so bad. Here it is:

A. Open all windows and send the family to the movies

B. Simmer chopped Onions in water to cover until soft

C. Add 1 T cooking oil per Onion ➡ a bit more won't hurt.

D. Cook over slow fire, scraping bottom once in a while when Onions stick. You may want to add bits of water to make scraping easier and soften the Onion pieces as they cook.

E. This process ends when the Onions sort of cling together like a golden paste in a bed of oil. The smell should be sweet and most appetizing.

40

INSTANT

Fried  Onions

If you don't have the time, or the inclination to prepare fried Onions the hard way, here is a fast and quite acceptable alternative:

For each  T dry instant minced Onions

use T cooking oil to fry until Onions are light gold

then add T water and simmer until water is absorbed and Onions are tender.

GINGER ~ carrot salad

4 large peeled carrots ➡ grated medium fine

Juice of **1** orange

1 T orange marmalade

1 T mayonnaise

1/2 c seedless raisins

1/8 t ginger

1/8 t

⬆ Mix the works
Serve chilled ➡

Garnish with candied ginger
and a little gob of marmalade

serves 6

42

Carrot Tzimes

1 T butter or margarine

2 T sugar

PINCH S

Fry until golden and bubbly

Add

hot water

1 C

1 lb. peeled carrots → cut in strips

Simmer on slow fire until water evaporates.

Tzimes Mehr'n, as this dish is Yiddishly called, is served as a side dish on festive occasions and also to get carrots into children who hate carrots.

serves 4

43

Papas a la

The province of Huancayo in the Central Andes is just as famous for Papas a la Huancaina as it is for its colorful Indian marketplace.

The recipe in this book is the Russo-Yiddish interpretation of this popular dish, to wit the addition of cottage cheese to the sauce and the mashing of the potatoes.

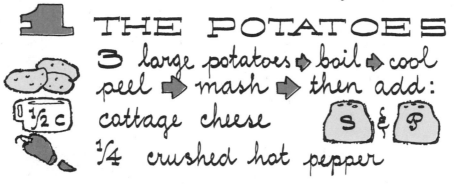

1 THE POTATOES

3 large potatoes ➡ boil ➡ cool peel ➡ mash ➡ then add:

½ c cottage cheese   S & P

¼ crushed hot pepper

➡ shape into 2" round balls
➡ arrange a tray full of these

hard-boiled egg slice
sauce ➡ be generous
olives
lettuce leaf
potato ball

44

Huancaina

2 THE SAUCE

→ In a mortar & pestle mash:

- **1** T onion
- ¼ clove garlic
- S & P
- ¾ hot pepper ▷ no seeds
- 2 T muenster or other "goaty" cheese
- **1** T lemon juice

Save contents till last ◀

→ In a separate bowl beat as you add in order:

- 2 egg yolks ▶ till light yellow
- ½ c oil, add a little at a time ▶ if it curdles see mayonnaise tip on p. 179.
- ½ c cottage cheese
- the contents of the mortar ◀

serves 6

Gefilte Malaiklaj

∽ filled potato patties ∽

3 potatoes, cooked, peeled & mashed

1 egg

2 T cracker meal

1 T shmaltz or oil

1   MIX WELL

SET ASIDE AND

2   MAKE THE FILLING

chopped fried chicken livers or left over meats.

piece chopped hot pepper

1 c

1 T shmaltz or oil

1 T fried onion (see p. 40)

2 T grieven (if you have any)

➡ Fry a few minutes.

➡ To the frying filling add: 25 cracker meal

➡ Mix well and take out of the fire

➡ While still hot add: **1** egg

➡ If mixture is too loose add cracker meal one spoon at a time

3   SHAPE THE PATTIES

➡ Form the potato mixture into 6 flat "cups", fill with filling, fold close and pat flat:

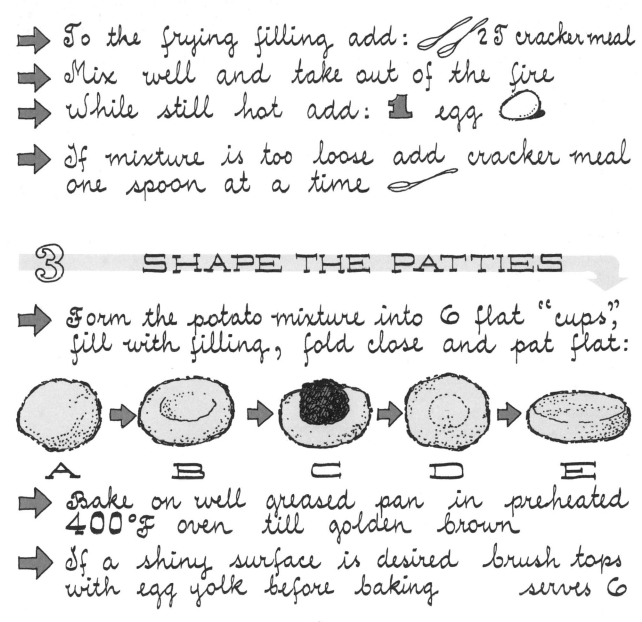

A   B   C   D   E

➡ Bake on well greased pan in preheated 400°F oven till golden brown

➡ If a shiny surface is desired brush tops with egg yolk before baking   serves 6

papas rellenas

∽ Gefilte malaiklaj Peruvian style ∾

1 Make a potato mixture same as for malaiklaj but use this spicier filling:

2 FILLING

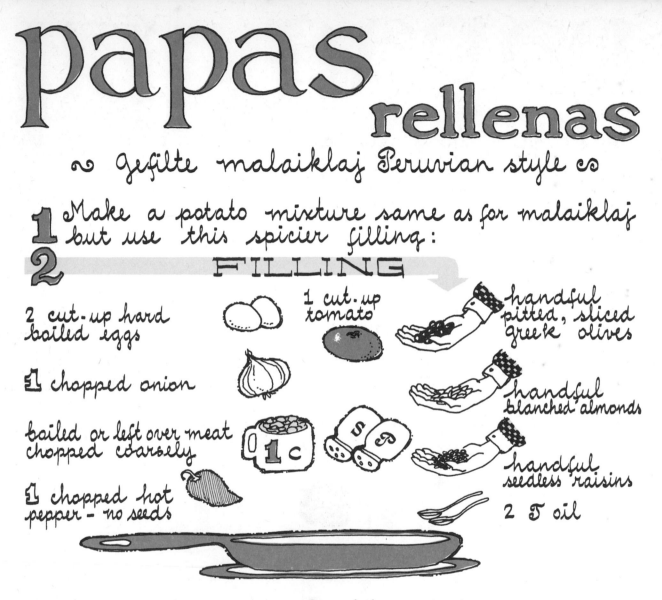

2 cut-up hard boiled eggs

1 chopped onion

boiled or left over meat chopped coarsely

1 chopped hot pepper - no seeds

1 cut-up tomato

1 c

S P

handful pitted, sliced greek olives

handful blanched almonds

handful seedless raisins

2 T oil

→ Fry all together and let cool before using to fill the patties

3 Proceed as for malaiklaj or dust the patties in flour and fry in a well-greased skillet.

papas
refritas

o~ *Refried potatoes* ~o

SLICE VERY THIN
DEEP FAT FRY
DO NOT BROWN
TAKE THEM OUT
LET COOL ON PAPER

INTO HOT OIL AGAIN
UNTIL BROWN
TAKE THEM OUT
DRAIN ON PAPER
SPRINKLE WITH SALT
SERVE AS A SNACK

hot oil

CAUSA

a 3 boiled potatoes ➡ cool ➡ peel ➡ mash

b In a blender blend:

juice of **1** orange
juice of **1** lemon
1 hot pepper ➡ no seeds
3 T oil + ¾ t S + ¼ t P

c Mix **a** + **b** and pat smooth over tray ➡ like so:

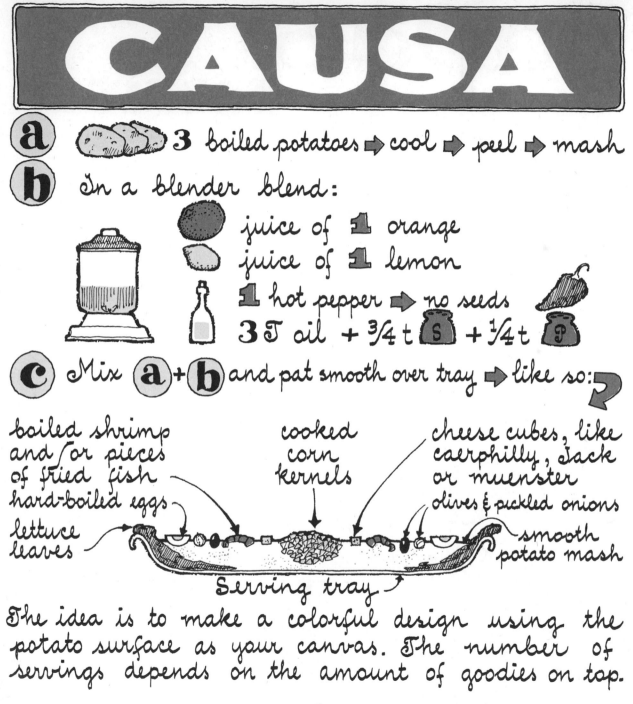

boiled shrimp and/or pieces of fried fish

hard-boiled eggs

lettuce leaves

cooked corn kernels

cheese cubes, like caerphilly, Jack or muenster

olives & pickled onions

smooth potato mash

Serving tray

The idea is to make a colorful design using the potato surface as your canvas. The number of servings depends on the amount of goodies on top.

PAPAS con CHARQUI

❦ Potatoes with Jerky ❧

This is an Indian dish traditionally made with ollucos, one of the more than twenty varieties of potatoes grown in Perú.

1 2 boiled potatoes ➡ peel ➡ cut in cubes

2 Break 4 large strips of beef jerky in pieces and soak in water for 30 min. ➡ drain and pound with a mallet till fibers separate

3 In a skillet fry:

oil 1/4 c

1 medium chopped onion

1 crushed garlic clove

1/8 t oregano

1/8 t parsley

1 sliced hot pepper - no seeds

S P

4 When onion starts to brown add the cubed potatoes and the jerky ➡ cook on low fire 20 min. ➡ stir occasionally and carefully ⬅

Serve side dish of sliced cucumbers and a bowl of yogurt   serves 2

BATIDO de frejoles

2 c red kidney beans

6 c water

piece salt pork
or 1 slice bacon

a Put all ingredients in a pot and bring to a boil

b Turn heat down ➡ simmer 2 ½ hrs. or until beans are tender.

c while beans simmer prepare the fried seasoning ➡ in a skillet brown lightly:

½ c oil

2 mashed garlic cloves

2 minced hot peppers — no seeds

d Mix: cooked beans, fried seasoning and ⑤ & ℗ to taste and ➡ Mash, crush, or blend in blender to a smooth mass.

e 1½ c grated Jack or mozzarella cheese

bean mixture

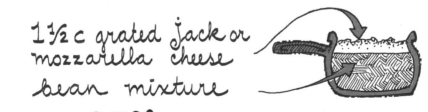

Bake in 250°F oven till beans are hot and cheese has melted, about 15 min.

To make it a truly Peruvian dinner serve batido with fried rice and bisté arrebozado with a side dish of fried bananas.   serves 6

Saltado de Col
⌘ Tossed Cabbage ⌘

1 3 strips bacon (or cubed piece of ham & 1 T oil) ➡ fry till crisp ➡ drain & set aside ➡

2 ➡ In the remaining fat fry, while you toss, until gold:

    2 c finely chopped cabbage

    1 minced onion

    1 chopped hot pepper - no seeds

3 ➡ Add: **1 c** water ➡ bring to a boil

4 ➡ Add: **½ c** long grain white rice

    ➡ shake pot ➡ cover ➡ turn heat to LOW

    ➡ don't touch for 20 min.

    ➡ out of fire leave covered 5 min.

5 ➡ Serve ➡ sprinkle with broken bits of crisp bacon (or pieces of ham)

    ➡ Offer soy sauce.   serves 3

Polita's Malisnik

~ a delicate cornmeal dish ~

1 pt yogurt

2 beaten eggs

7 oz. evaporated milk

1½ t melted butter

½ pt. small curd cottage cheese

a Mix

cornmeal ¾ c

flour ¼ c

sugar ¼ c

1 t S

½ t baking powder

b Mix

c 3 t melted butter, then mix **a**+**b** & pour in

warm pyrex dish

d Bake → 400°F — Reduce to → 350°F

30 min.   30 min.

Serve hot with side dish of chilled sour cream.   serves 6

HUMITAS

Humitas are delicate in flavor and texture and are a complement to any meat dish.
Serve in their individual packages and let each one unwrap his own.

1

cut off stems

save husks
wash & dry

grate kernels

discard silk

⬆ 4 RATHER MATURE CORN COBS

2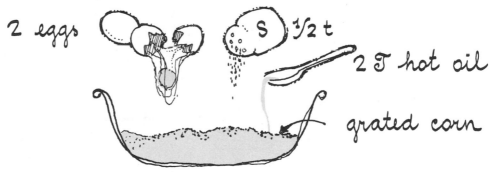

2 eggs · S · ½ t · 2 T hot oil · grated corn

If the mixture is too runny add 1 or 2 T cracker meal, otherwise omit. ➡ go pack

3 PACKING DETAILS

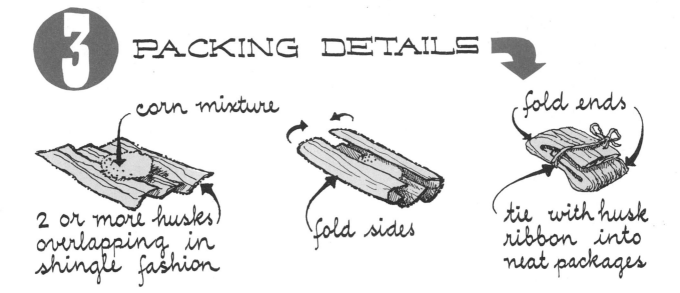

corn mixture

2 or more husks overlapping in shingle fashion

fold sides

fold ends

tie with husk ribbon into neat packages

4 STEAM FOR 30 MIN.

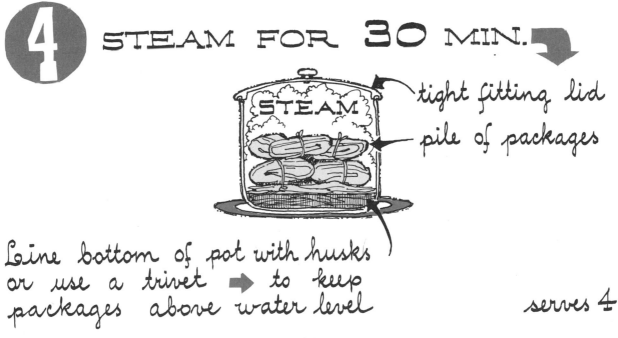

STEAM

tight fitting lid

pile of packages

Line bottom of pot with husks or use a trivet ➡ to keep packages above water level

serves 4

PEPIÁN

Mild version

grate **4** cobs of corn - about **2 c**

S **½ t**

½ c milk

Cook 10 min. or till thickened

Spicy version

½ chopped hot pepper - no seeds

crushed ½ garlic clove

1 T oil

Brown lightly and ➡ add to cooking grated corn mixture

Serve pepián instead of rice or potatoes.

serves **4**

Eggplant Guiso

1 large eggplant ▶ skin and all
 ▶ cut into ½" slices
 ▶ soak them in cold salted water ½ Hr.
 ▶ Rinse ▶ dry ▶ fry in hot oil a few min. each side
 ▶ drain ▶ set aside ⟶

sliced green pepper ⟍   ⟋ cut up tomato · no skin · no seeds
                              ←— dash garlic salt
                        2 T oil

▶ Fry till golden   ▶ then add ⎰ fried eggplant
                                 ⎱ ¼C water
                                   S & P
                                   ⅛ t paprika

▶ Turn eggplant slices several times gingerly ◀
▶ Cook till eggplant is tender and sauce is not watery
   but shiny , about 30 min.
▶ Serve hot or cold ▶ Makes good meatless sandwiches

PITA FALAFEL

This Middle Eastern sandwich is a favorite in Israel, where street vendors excel in preparing this traditional unleavened bread stuffed with garbanzo balls and generously topped with hot sauce.

❧ Unleavened bread ❧

flattish bowl → water 7/8c — S 1/4 t → 1 c whole wheat flour

1 Work with hands until you have a smooth, elastic, non-sticky dough → about 5 min.

2 Make 4 equal balls → about 1½" diameter

3 On lightly oiled board roll each very thin and very round

4 Deep fat fry till puffed and golden (or bake at 425°F for 5 min. on rack)

5 Split top to open and stuff with garbanzo balls → garnish with hot sauce

❧ garbanzo balls ❧

15 oz. can drained garbanzos
or 2 c cooked garbanzos
➡ grind, do not mash ➡ use blender or meat grinder

Add: **2** beaten eggs
1 T finely minced onion
S ¼ t & P ⅛ t
3 T matzo meal
➡ Let rest 10 min.
➡ Make **1**" diameter balls ➡ about 16
deep fat fry till golden ➡ drain

❧ Hot sauce ❧

2 sliced onions

2 T olive oil
1 t chopped parsley

2 sliced hot peppers no seeds

⅓ c wine vinegar

Marinate **1** hr.   serves 4

61

Beef Shanks in Peanut Sauce

1

1 1/2 lb. beef shanks
→ boil in water to cover until tender
→ set shanks aside →
→ skim fat from broth & save (the broth) →

2

→ Brown shanks with: chopped hot pepper
S P
1/4 t oregano
2 T oil

3

→ Add: 1/2 c broth
1/4 c peanut butter

→ Cook & stir a few more minutes
→ Serve with boiled potatoes.   serves 4 to 6

Vaca al Vino

∽ Beef with almonds in sweet wine ∽

1 crushed garlic clove
few slices chorizo
piece salt pork or bacon
1 T oil

1 Brown ⬆

2 Add:

1 ½ lb. beef stew meat

1 cut-up tomato

6 pearl onions

¼ t oregano

1 c water

½ c sweet red wine

Simmer covered till meat almost done, about 45 min.

3 Add:

2 T red wine vinegar

½ c blanched almonds

½ c seedless raisins

Simmer uncovered until sauce is rich and meat is tender ➡ about 20 min.   serves 6

PRAKES

⌁ Sweet and Sour Stuffed Cabbage ⌁

a Large cabbage leaves ➡ dip in boiling water till flexible enough to serve as wrapping

b Filling: **1** lb. lean ground beef

2 T raw white rice

1 T oil

1 T fried onion (see p. 40)

1 T

3/4 t

1 egg or **1** extra T oil

1/8 t sour salt

c Sauce: 2 T oil

1 T fried onion (see p. 40)

2 peeled tomatoes - no seeds

1/4 c

1 t

1/4 t sour salt

Taste Test ⬇ Touch mixture to your tongue for proper balance of: { sweet salt sour

⬅ Fry till it looks like a golden marmalade

64

d <u>Construction:</u>

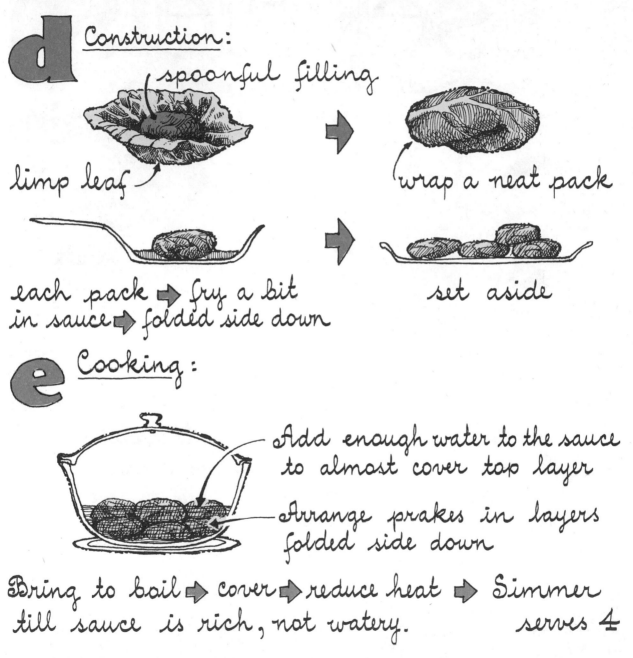

spoonful filling

limp leaf →   wrap a neat pack

each pack → fry a bit   set aside
in sauce → folded side down

e <u>Cooking:</u>

Add enough water to the sauce
to almost cover top layer

Arrange prakes in layers
folded side down

Bring to boil → cover → reduce heat → Simmer
till sauce is rich, not watery.   serves 4

EssekFleish

~ Sweet and Sour Stew ~

1 lb. beef stew

1 onion

OIL

SUGAR 1/4 c

1 tomato no skin - no seeds

S 1/2 t

2 T

SOUR SALT 1/4 t

1. Cook meat & whole onion in water to cover till meat is almost tender.
2. Drain meat ➡ save liquid ➡ discard the onion ➡
3. In the oil fry the meat ✚ all other ingredients.
      When sauce is amber, like marmalade:
4. Add the saved liquid ✚ enough water to cover meat.
5. Simmer over medium heat till sauce is reduced to a rich consistency.
6. Taste test for: ➡ Sweet ➡ Salt ➡ Sour

Serve with homemade noodles or steamed rice.   serves 4

picadillo

～ Minced Stuff ～

The quantities in this recipe are not given because it is in the nature of picadillo never to be quite the same.

 Mince leftover meats, whatever they are, and fry them in oil or bacon fat together with:

crushed garlic clove

some seedless raisins

a few Greek olives

cut up tomato without skin or seeds

small piece hot pepper

cut-up hard-boiled eggs

S & P

When it is all done add:

1 T red wine vinegar

Toss quickly and serve with rice, potatoes or chunks of French bread.

SALSA DOS POR TRES

~ Sauce 2×3 → a speedy spaghetti sauce ~

1 In hot pan fry **2** lb. crumbled ground beef, tossing quickly → don't let it brown → drain → set aside →
→ discard remaining fat ←

2 In the pan put:

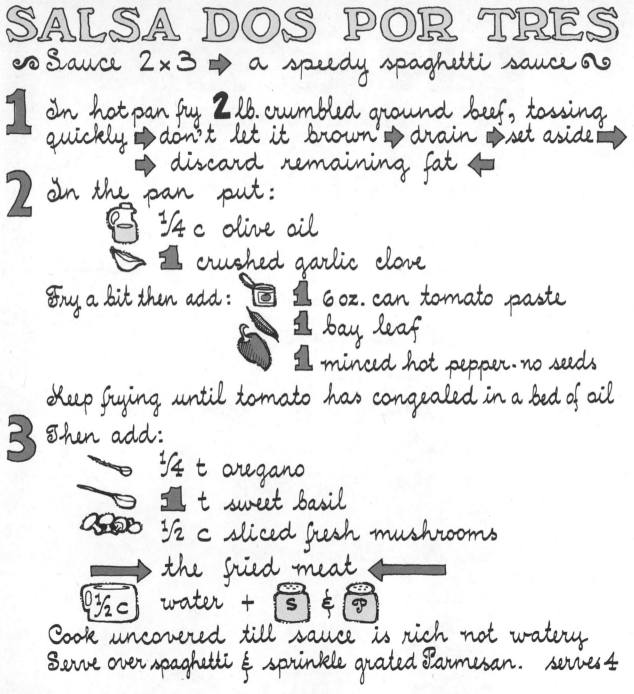

¼ c olive oil

1 crushed garlic clove

Fry a bit then add:

1 6 oz. can tomato paste

1 bay leaf

1 minced hot pepper - no seeds

Keep frying until tomato has congealed in a bed of oil

3 Then add:

¼ t oregano

1 t sweet basil

½ c sliced fresh mushrooms

→ the fried meat ←

1½ c water + S & P

Cook uncovered till sauce is rich not watery
Serve over spaghetti & sprinkle grated Parmesan. serves 4

Fried Rice

1 c white rice
1 T oil
½ t ⬚S

Brown rice in oil & salt then add [2c] boiling water
Cover ➡ lower heat to low ➡ cook 20 min.
Out of fire ➡ let sit covered 5 min. ➡ Serve

Bisté Arrebozado
~ chicken fried steak ~

1 Beef or lamb steaks
➡ pound very thin ➡
(or use lean ground meat patted thin)

2 Dust the steaks in mixture of:
bread crumbs + S + P + garlic salt

3 Dip them in beaten egg

4 Fry them in oil till golden

5 Serve with fried rice and for an extra
treat add a gob of batido de frejoles.

pseudo
pastrami

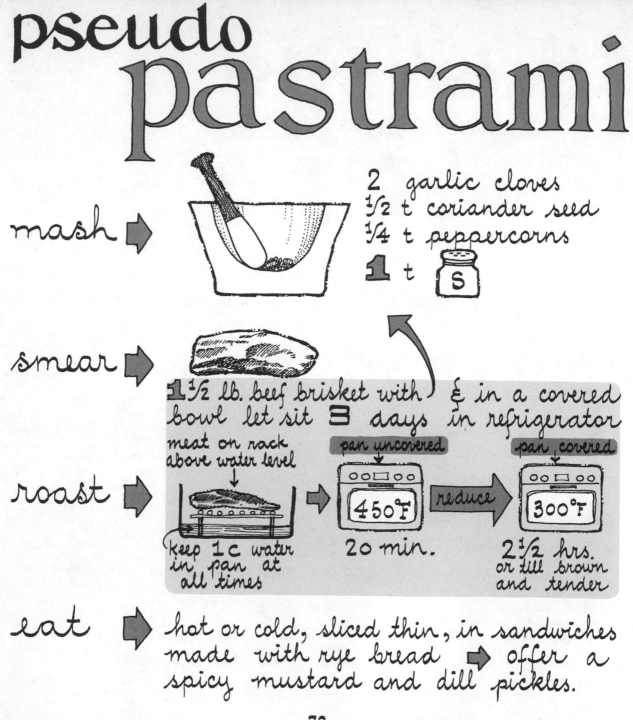

mash ➡

2 garlic cloves
1/2 t coriander seed
1/4 t peppercorns
1 t [S]

smear ➡

roast ➡

1 1/2 lb. beef brisket with & in a covered bowl let sit 3 days in refrigerator

meat on rack above water level

keep 1 c water in pan at all times

pan uncovered
450°F
20 min.

reduce

pan covered
300°F
2 1/2 hrs. or till brown and tender

eat ➡ hot or cold, sliced thin, in sandwiches made with rye bread ➡ offer a spicy mustard and dill pickles.

Mechado

Mechar means to put mechas or strips of fat pork into other meats such as fowl or beef, which really has nothing to do with this recipe.

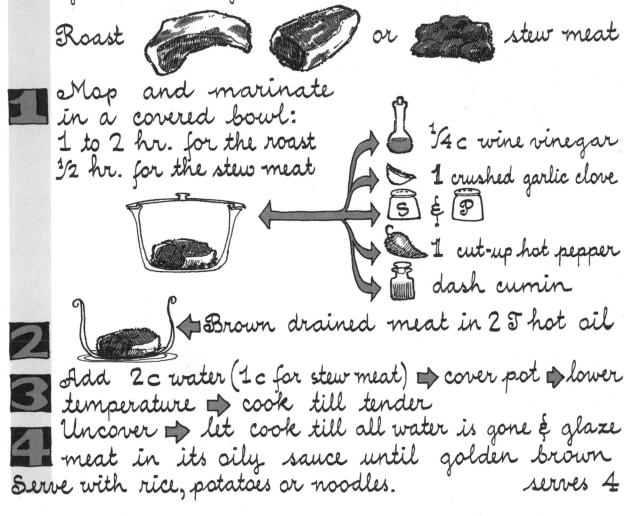

Roast or stew meat

1 Mop and marinate in a covered bowl:
1 to 2 hr. for the roast
½ hr. for the stew meat

¼ c wine vinegar
1 crushed garlic clove
S & P
1 cut-up hot pepper
dash cumin

Brown drained meat in 2 T hot oil

2

3 Add 2 c water (1 c for stew meat) ➡ cover pot ➡ lower temperature ➡ cook till tender

4 Uncover ➡ let cook till all water is gone & glaze meat in its oily sauce until golden brown

Serve with rice, potatoes or noodles.   serves 4

Pelotitas

Jewish meatballs in Peruvian Sauce

➡ Combine:

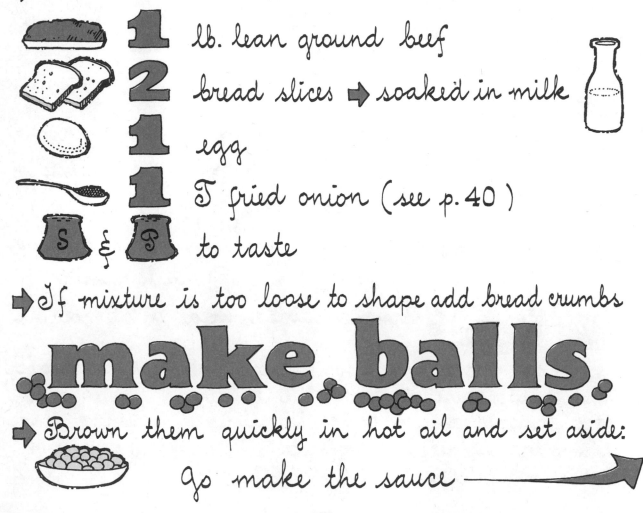

1 lb. lean ground beef

2 bread slices ➡ soaked in milk

1 egg

1 T fried onion (see p. 40)

S & **P** to taste

➡ If mixture is too loose to shape add bread crumbs

make balls

➡ Brown them quickly in hot oil and set aside:

go make the sauce ⟶

Sauce ➡ **Fry well:**

crushed garlic clove

chopped hot pepper

2 cut-up tomatoes
(no skin - no seeds)

1 T fried onion
(see p. 40)

2 T oil

➡ **Add:** **1** T red wine & stir a bit

1 c water & heat to boil & then to simmer

➡ **Add:** meat balls

½ c whole mushrooms

½ c fresh peas

S & P

PINCH nutmeg & **PINCH** oregano

➡ Simmer till sauce is rich and oily and the peas are done.

➡ Serve thus: ➡
pelatitas

sauce

rice molded in a buttered cup

serves 4

Saltado de Hígado
～Tossed Liver～

1 **1** sliced onion   **1** sliced hot pepper-no seeds
1 T vinegar   ¼ c water

- Cook until dry ➡ then set aside ➡
- Deep fat fry **1** potato cut in cubes 🥔 set aside ➡

2 **1** lb. beef liver ➡ remove ducts & cut in **1"** cubes
➡ soak in enough water to cover plus **1** T vinegar
for 30 min. ➡ rinse ➡ dry & proceed:

liver cubes   ← pinch garlic salt
¼ c oil

(hot fire)

- Fry tossing quickly till brown

3 Add the cooked onion stuff plus (S) & (P) &
toss around a few minutes, then add the
fried potatoes ➡ fry & toss a bit more.
- Serve with steamed rice.   serves 4

Golden Tongue

- Scald **1** fresh beef tongue in boiling water a few minutes till skin quite white.
- Peel by scraping with knife.
- Scald again on tenacious spots (the fresher the tongue the easier it peels) ➡ Rinse ⬅

1 orange slice, skin & all
1 carrot
S ½ t & PINCH P

cold H_2O to cover half the tongue.

- Bring to boil.
- Cover & reduce heat to medium ➡ turn tongue a few times to cook evenly.
- When tongue is tender (about 2½ to 3 hrs.), uncover.
- When water has evaporated, brown tongue in its own oils until deep gold.
- Serve hot with rice or potatoes, or refrigerate and use for sandwiches on French bread with mayonnaise and lettuce.
- One large tongue will serve about 6 to 8.

In the 1930's and 40's, when we were children, the best anticuchos would invariably be found in establishments run by a single person, in courtyards behind those wooden gates which abound in Lima. No sign ever marked these places, the smell permeating the streets was enough.

Besides anticuchos, the fare normally consisted of boiled corn on the cob, fried sweet potato slices and picarones, a type of donut steeped in syrup (see p.164).

Anticuchos

1 cow's heart cut in **1**" cubes
➤ remove fat, veins and ligaments
➤ wash & drain & marinate
in ➡
for

2
Hrs

¼c wine vinegar
S & P
chopped hot pepper
Pinch Cumin
crushed garlic clove

➤ Skewer ⬤▬⬤⬤⬤⬤▬ cubes
➤ Barbecue on charcoal over a grate
➤ Baste frequently with a mixture of
oil and crushed hot pepper.

In Perú the basting is done with
a feather.

seco de cabrito

Seco is a northern dish traditionally made with goat meat; but it can be successfully made with lamb or beef. It is hard to understand why this dish is called seco, or "dry" in Spanish, since it is a very juicy concoction.

a

SMASH in a mortar & pestle or blender:

1 bunch culantro {Chinese parsley}

2 garlic cloves

1 hot pepper ➡ no seeds

1 T cooking oil

1/8 t ➡

3/4 t ⬅

keep the mash until later

b Fry: **2** lb. goat stew meat in **1/4** c cooking oil ➡ till well browned

c Add: **4** cut-up green onions ➡ tails & all

1 cut-up tomato and

the contents of the mortar

d Fry a few minutes more ➡ then add:

1 c water

1/2 c fresh green peas

15 oz. can new potatoes

e Cover pot ➡ lower temperature ➡ cook until meat is almost done ➡ uncover pot and keep cooking until sauce is like heavy cream ➡ SERVE with rice garnished with some of the green sauce.   serves 4

Tamarindo
~ Tamarind ~

The streets of Perú have always abounded in vendors of sundry tasty items. When we were children I remember spending all our pocket money on such delicacies as turrón de Doña Pepa, a multilayered pastry dripping with honey; empanadas, pasties filled with meat; máchica, a mixture of toasted corn flour and sugar, which was tricky to eat unless you held your breath; and countless others. But our favorites by far were aceitunas de botija, plump purple olives in brine; and the puckering pulp of tamarind.

In the United States tamarindo is often available in stores that cater to Spanish speaking cooks.

Tamarindo has been questionably credited for being good against fever and unquestionably credited for its laxative properties.

Norita's Chancho con Tamarindo
~ Pork in Tamarind Sauce ~

1 2 lb. lean pork roast ➡ cut in cubes
➡ brown them in hot ungreased pan

2 Lower heat & add:
1 t each ➡ honey
soy sauce
brandy
& ½ t S

➡ fry a few minutes tossing around

3 Add: 4 T water & 2 T orange juice
➡ cover and simmer till tender ➡ SET ASIDE

4 GO MAKE THE SAUCE
Tamarind Sauce

2 T tamarind pulp - no seeds
2 T water
1 T white vinegar
2 t honey

➡ Cook till dissolved ➡ strain ➡ add:
2 t cornstarch dissolved in 1/4 c water
1 minced hot pepper - no seeds
1 T soy sauce
3 pearl onions sliced thin   S & P

5 ➡ Cook till thickened but fluid ➡ if too thick add water
➡ Add the cooked pork ➡ toss and cook 1 min. more.
➡ Serve with steamed rice.   serves 4

gutifarras

A gutifarra is a take-out sandwich of cold pork with an onion sauce, sold by small establishments at summer resorts near Lima. The best ones I remember are the ones we used to get in La Punta, which as its name implies is an extremely narrow and long peninsula, 30 minutes from Lima.

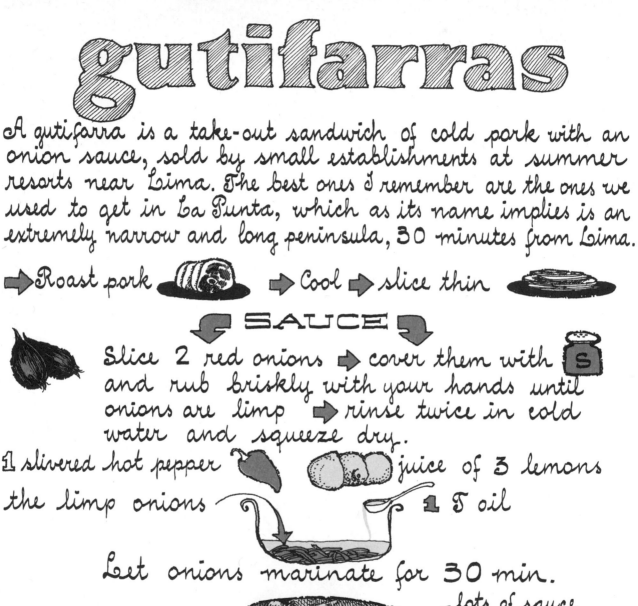

➡ Roast pork ➡ Cool ➡ slice thin

➡ SAUCE ⬅

Slice 2 red onions ➡ cover them with **S** and rub briskly with your hands until onions are limp ➡ rinse twice in cold water and squeeze dry.

1 slivered hot pepper   juice of 3 lemons

the limp onions   1 T oil

Let onions marinate for 30 min.

GUTIFARRA ➡

lots of sauce
cold pork slices
lettuce leaf
French bun

Scraping a Chicken?

Here I must confess to a habit which I inherited from my mother, who inherited it from her mother in the Old Country.

Before doing anything with a chicken carefully scrape the entire body with a knife until the thin yellow layer that covers most of the skin has been thoroughly removed, rinse the chicken and proceed with dish preparation.

Once you witness that which you scrape off, you will either give up eating chicken or become a confirmed chicken scraper.

Yet, I am really somewhat loath to recommend that you start with this ritual since I have tried, in vain, to ascertain any but the visual reason for it, or even what it is that I am so diligently removing.

But, true to habits, I very likely will continue scraping chickens until the day I become a vegetarian.

grieven &

chicken skin cracklings   and

If you have been making grieven by frying skin in melting chunks of chicken fat you are in for a pleasant surprise. Your new grieven will be plump, light and of a milder taste.

1 Wash chicken skin and chunks of fat in cold water
2 On chopping block cut skin in **1"** squares
3 Scrape the fat off the membranes covering the chunks

➡ DISCARD THE MEMBRANES ⬅

4 In a heavy pot put skin squares, scraped fat and cold water to cover and bring to a boil
5 Lower heat and simmer uncovered until all water is evaporated and grieven start frying in the melted shmaltz. Continue to fry, scraping often with spoon to avoid sticking to pan.
6 Grieven are ready when they "talk": take a fork and gently tap floating grieven with the back of the tongs, so: ➡

TAP ⬇   ⬇ TAP

shmaltz

rendered chicken fat

7 Bring your ear to about **6"** from the grieven, if they sound ch - ch - ch they are ready. If they emit a dull thud sound they need more cooking.
Remove the drained grieven to a flat plate and sprinkle them generously with salt.

8 Salt the remaining shmaltz and store in the refrigerator in a container capped with a lid poked full of holes (this prevents its becoming rancid). A pinch of salt per cup of shmaltz is enough.

Shmaltz is the traditional cooking fat in Jewish dishes. It is also quite palatable as a spread on rye bread; and mixed with mashed potatoes instead of butter. My grandmother used to make shmaltz from geese which she fattened outrageously for the purpose. Grieven are tasty tid-bits and are used in the preparation of such dishes as varenikes, a type of ravioli, in which grieven are mixed with the potatoes or casha used in the filling.

HELZEL

❀ Stuffed chicken neck skins ❀

STUFFING PROCEDURE

A Sew closed one end of chicken neck skin making a long pocket (use white thread)

B Fill loosely with stuffing # **1** or # **2** ➡

C Sew closed the other end.

D Roast with the rest of the chicken, whatever recipe you are using.

STUFFING # **1** ➡ Dry ⬅

3 T chicken fat (straight out of the chicken)
Scrape the fat ➡ discard covering membranes
or substitute shmaltz or simply oil.

6 T flour (S) & (P)

➡ Mix all to a heavy paste ⬅

➡ # STUFFING # **2** ➡ Eggy

1 egg ➡ beat with:

1 T oil
Add: (S) & (P)

2 slices stale but not dry
bread ➡ crumble between
hands or chop them in
blender.

➡ Mix all to a wet pulp ⬅

When making stuffed turkey or chicken you can
use either of these stuffings inside body cavity of bird.

Chicken Guiso

1 One cut-up fryer ➡ wash well and dry her

2 Fry in hot oil ➡ till gold on every side

3 Take out the pieces and set them aside ➡

4 In the remaining oil fry till lightly browned:

1 sliced green pepper

1 chopped onion

1 crushed garlic clove

1 sliced carrot

1 peeled tomato - no seeds either

1 chopped hot pepper - no seeds

5 Now add:

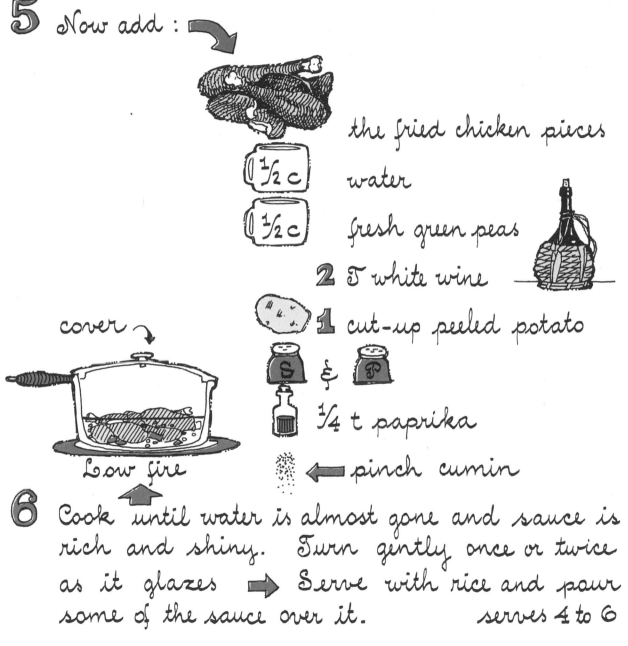

the fried chicken pieces

½ c water

½ c fresh green peas

2 T white wine

1 cut-up peeled potato

S & P

¼ t paprika

← pinch cumin

cover →

Low fire

6 Cook until water is almost gone and sauce is rich and shiny. Turn gently once or twice as it glazes ➡ Serve with rice and pour some of the sauce over it.   serves 4 to 6

Paella

This dish was imported to Perú from Spain and it lends itself to infinite variations. This one is based on the paella made in Valencia.

1 Brown cut-up fryer chicken in 1/4 c oil, drain and set aside ➡

2 In the oil fry till brown:

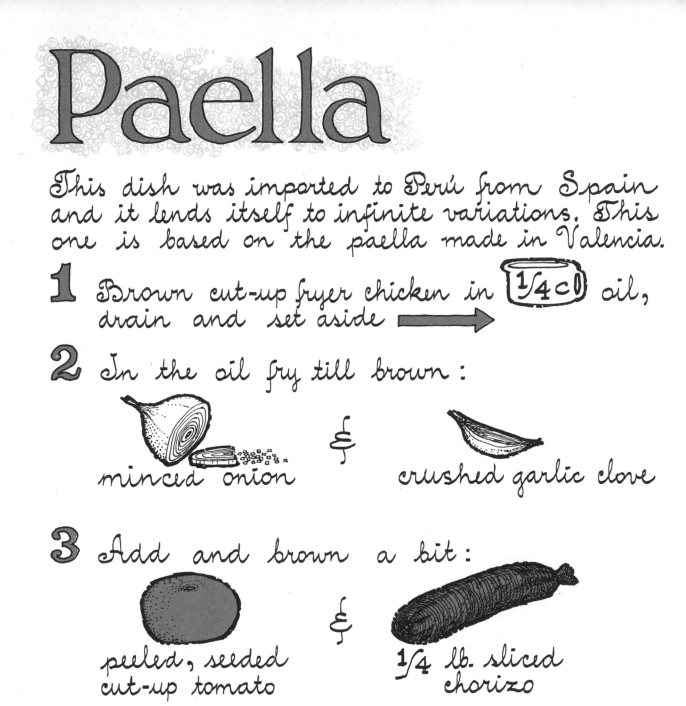

minced onion   &   crushed garlic clove

3 Add and brown a bit:

peeled, seeded cut-up tomato   &   1/4 lb. sliced chorizo

4 Add the fried chicken and:

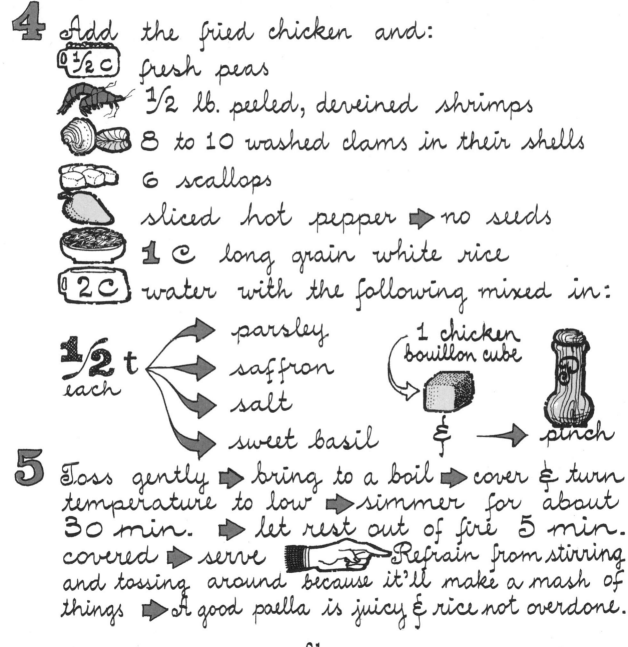

½ C fresh peas

½ lb. peeled, deveined shrimps

8 to 10 washed clams in their shells

6 scallops

sliced hot pepper ➡ no seeds

1 C long grain white rice

2 C water with the following mixed in:

½ t each ➡ parsley
➡ saffron
➡ salt
➡ sweet basil

1 chicken bouillon cube & ➡ pinch

5 Toss gently ➡ bring to a boil ➡ cover & turn temperature to low ➡ simmer for about 30 min. ➡ let rest out of fire 5 min. covered ➡ serve ☞ Refrain from stirring and tossing around because it'll make a mash of things ➡ A good paella is juicy & rice not overdone.

Chicken à l'Orange
(pronounce Frenchy)

1 1 T each →
- margarine
- grated orange peel
- honey
- white wine

3

S   P

2 1 t each →
- soy sauce
- ginger

4 2½ lb. frying chicken ⇨ mop with: **1** + **2** + **3**

30 minutes later

5 Lay drained chicken pieces on baking dish

6 Bake in preheated 400°F oven ⇨ 20 min.

7 Reduce heat to 300°F ⇨ till brown
(Turn & baste & fool around at will)

8 When you think it's all done: squeeze juice of
1 orange on top of chicken & bake **5** min. more.

SERVE WITH STEAMED RICE   serves 6

Baylick Fish

gefilte fish with no fish

2 lb. chicken breasts ➡ no skin ➡ no bones
➡ no membranes

Now, using the chicken breasts instead of fish proceed as with Gefilte Fish (see p. 36)

You may need an extra ½ t Ⓢ & some Ⓟ

serves 4 to 6

3 Hens in 1 Pot

→ Birds must be plucked & cleaned of course.
→ Wash, dry and mop inside & out with this emulsion ⮧

Peruvians use pichones or doves → you can use Cornish game hens.

2 T shmaltz or soft margarine
1 crushed garlic clove
2 T wine vinegar + S & P

→ Set them aside and go make the stuffing

→ The Stuffing ← Mix:

2 slices French bread soaked in milk & squeezed

1 c minced cooked ham

2 egg yolks

2 t grated Parmesan cheese

2 sprigs parsley

¼ t grated lemon peel

¼ t crushed hot pepper

S ¼ t & ¼ t P plus a PINCH nutmeg

1 Stuff bird cavities ➡ sew holes with white thread & tie legs (each pair separately)

2 In a pot lightly brown each bird all over ➡ remove from oil and set aside   ¼c oil

3 To the oil add : 2 T tomato paste 1c water ¼t sweet basil ½ laurel leaf   S & P

4 Now set the **3** birds in the pot, cover & over medium heat cook till tender ➡ about 1 hr.

5 Uncover ➡ baste well ➡ cook till you have a rich juicy sauce.

Serve with humitas or mashed potatoes and a tossed green salad.   serves 6

arroz con pato

The northern town of Chiclayo, where I was born, happens to be famous for this dish which is usually referred to as Arroz con Pato a la Chiclayana. It is a rich meal in one pot. Its green color, unique taste and fragrance are due to the generous use of fresh culantro (cilantro in Mexican shops, Chinese parsley in Chinatown and coriander leaf in gardening books).

1 1 bunch culantro & 1/4 c water ➡ mash, crush or blend to a pulp ➡ set aside ➡

2 1/2 duck ➡ cut up (use liver for something else)
➡ brown pieces in 1 T oil
➡ take out & set aside ➡

3 In the pot fry:

remaining fat ↴

1 small chopped onion (my mother omitted it)

1 cut-up tomato - no skin - no seeds

1 crushed hot pepper - no seeds

1 crushed garlic clove

96

4 After a few minutes add: the culantro pulp 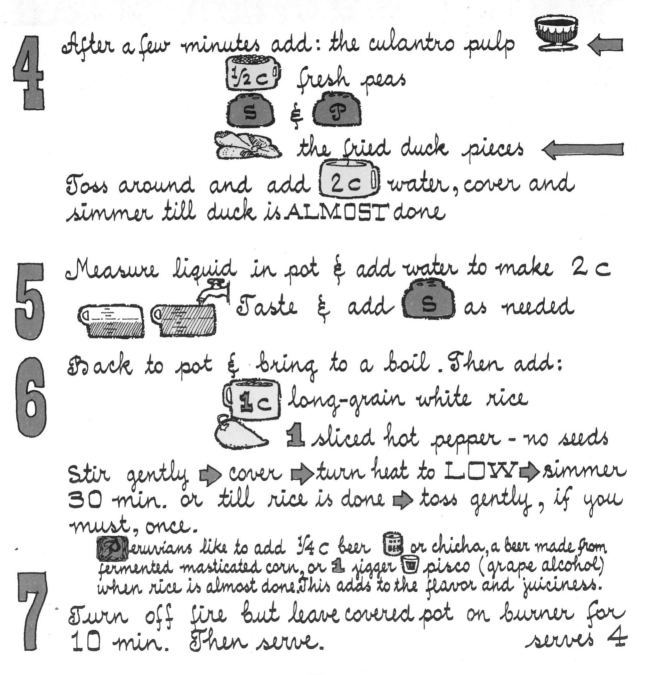 ⬅

½ c fresh peas

S & P

the fried duck pieces ⬅

Toss around and add 2 c water, cover and simmer till duck is ALMOST done

5 Measure liquid in pot & add water to make 2 c

Taste & add S as needed

6 Back to pot & bring to a boil. Then add:

1 c long-grain white rice

1 sliced hot pepper - no seeds

Stir gently ➡ cover ➡ turn heat to LOW ➡ simmer 30 min. or till rice is done ➡ toss gently, if you must, once.

Peruvians like to add ¼ c beer or chicha, a beer made from fermented masticated corn, or 1 jigger pisco (grape alcohol) when rice is almost done. This adds to the flavor and juiciness.

7 Turn off fire but leave covered pot on burner for 10 min. Then serve.   serves 4

Polita's Pato con Piña

Pineapple Duck

1 lb. duck meat → cut in thin strips
(no skin → no fat)

1 t soy sauce

2 T cornstarch

3 T oil

1 garlic clove

to taste

1 T sugar

1 c juice from can of pineapple

3 T catsup

pinch ginger

10 small pearl onions

1 red sweet pepper → cut in thin strips

5 slices canned pineapple → cut in pieces.

1 Mop duck strips with soy sauce and dust them with **1** T of the cornstarch.

2 Brown them in 2 T hot oil ➡ about 15 min.

3 Remove duck strips & set them aside ⟶

4 To the pot add **1** T oil & in it fry the garlic clove until golden ➡ discard the fried garlic.

5 Return duck to pot & add (S), sugar, pineapple juice, catsup & ginger ➡ Cook, covered, on medium heat for about 30 min. or until tender.

6 Add onions, sweet pepper & pineapple pieces; cook & stir gently a couple of minutes.

7 Add the other T cornstarch diluted in 1/2 c water; stir and cook until thickened.

Taste for sweet & salt

Serve with steamed rice.   serves 4

Picante de Cuy

Made with Rabbit instead

Cuy or South American cavy is the ancestor of the domestic Guinea pig and has been in the Peruvian menu since pre-Incan times. The meat of the cuy is not unlike that of rabbit in texture but in flavor it is somewhat stronger than rabbit. Picante literally means "hot" and that it is.

a Put a 2 lb. cut-up rabbit (use liver for something else) in ③ c cold water with ① t ⑤ ➡ bring to a boil ➡ cover ➡ turn heat down & simmer till tender.

SET ASIDE ➡

b In the meantime in a mortar & pestle mash:

2 hot peppers ➡ no veins ➡ no seeds

¼ t oregano

¼ t peppercorns

① T water

PINCH cumin

100

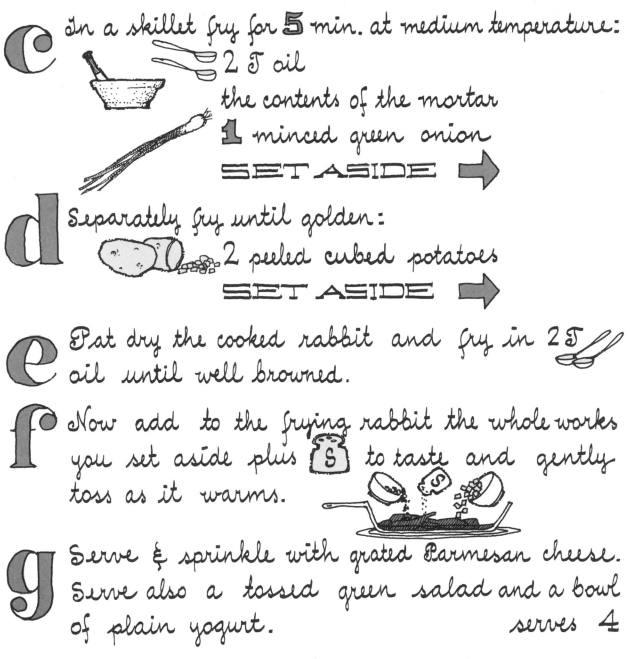

c In a skillet fry for **5** min. at medium temperature:

2 T oil

the contents of the mortar

1 minced green onion

SET ASIDE ➡

d Separately fry until golden:

2 peeled cubed potatoes

SET ASIDE ➡

e Pat dry the cooked rabbit and fry in 2 T oil until well browned.

f Now add to the frying rabbit the whole works you set aside plus **S** to taste and gently toss as it warms.

g Serve & sprinkle with grated Parmesan cheese. Serve also a tossed green salad and a bowl of plain yogurt.

serves 4

Ñoques, Noodles & Dumplings
and other doughy things

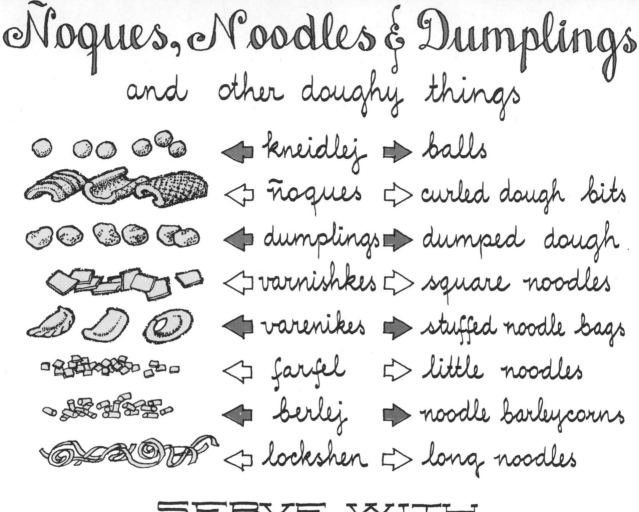

kneidlej → balls

ñoques ⇨ curled dough bits

dumplings → dumped dough

varnishkes ⇨ square noodles

varenikes → stuffed noodle bags

farfel ⇨ little noodles

berlej → noodle barleycorns

lockshen ⇨ long noodles

SERVE WITH

Soups and broths
Meat and meat sauces
Shmaltz and grieven
Butter and cottage cheese
Sour cream or cream cheese
Plain old butter and salt.

Matzo meal Kneidlej

1 Measure  3 eggs in a cup

2 Measure an equal amount of water

3 Beat the eggs then add:

  1 T oil

  the measured water

  3/4 t

  1 c matzo meal

4 MIX and let rest in refrigerator **15** min.

5 Shape the mixture into about **16** balls   **1 ½"** round.

6 Cook in gently boiling, salted water in a covered pot for **30** min.

➡ drain & serve

Traditionally served in clear chicken broth.

ñoques

- **1c** boiled, peeled, mashed potatoes
- **1c** cooked toasted cream of wheat ← see
- 2 eggs
- **S** ½ t
- **1¼c** flour ➡ give or take a bit

COOKED TOASTED CREAM OF WHEAT

1 T oil ¼t **S** **¼c** cream of wheat

Fry, stirring until golden.

then add ¾ c boiling water, lower heat & stir & cook a few minutes until done.

Stuff is done when it pulls away from sides of pan.

This cream of wheat also makes a fine side dish to meat by adding fried onions after it is cooked.

THE MAKING OF THE ÑOQUES

1 Mix all ingredients except flour.

2 Add the flour and work into a firm clay-like dough.

3 On a well-floured board, roll dough into long fingers as thick as your little finger.

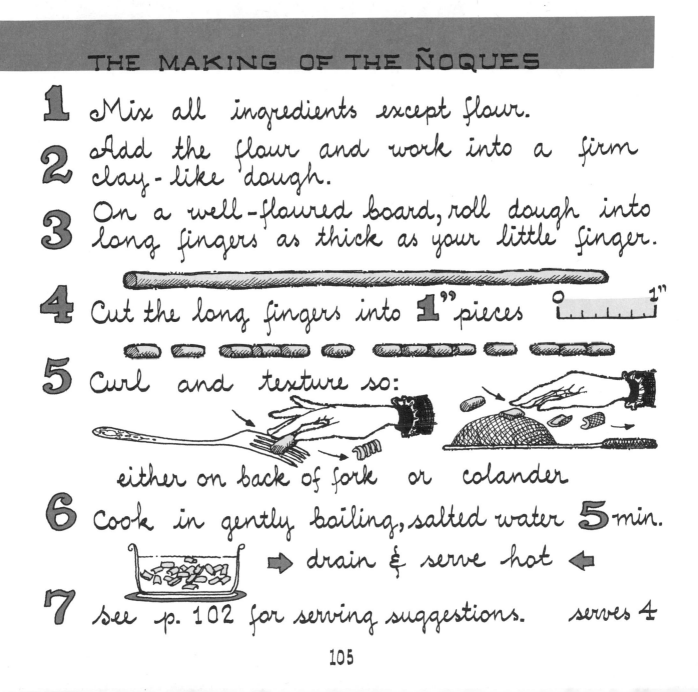

4 Cut the long fingers into **1"** pieces

5 Curl and texture so:

either on back of fork   or   colander

6 Cook in gently boiling, salted water **5** min.

➡ drain & serve hot ⬅

7 see p. 102 for serving suggestions.   serves 4

POTATO dumplings

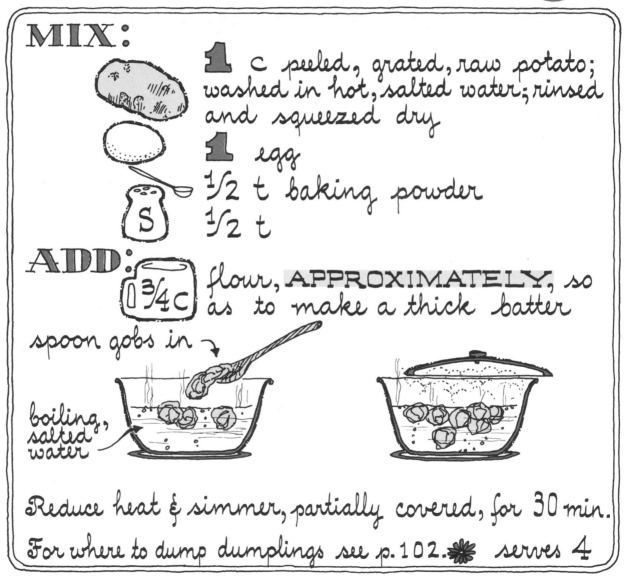

MIX:

1 c peeled, grated, raw potato; washed in hot, salted water; rinsed and squeezed dry

1 egg

½ t baking powder

½ t

ADD:

¾ c flour, APPROXIMATELY, so as to make a thick batter

spoon gobs in ⟶

boiling, salted water

Reduce heat & simmer, partially covered, for 30 min.

For where to dump dumplings see p.102. ❀ serves 4

CHEESE dumplings

doughy things

MIX:

1 pt. baker's or farmer's cheese, passed through sieve. (If you use cottage cheese, add more flour for firmness)

2 eggs

¼ t S

½ c cracker meal

½ c flour

SCULPT: Place a spoonful in wet hand and shape into finger-length receptacles

DROP into boiling, salted water

Reduce heat & simmer, partially covered, for 5 min. Drain gently, because they are delicate.

Serve with butter or sour cream and salt. ❀ serves 6

VARNISHKES

1 Make a noodle dough, by mixing:

    2 eggs

    ¼ t S

    1½ c flour **APPROXIMATELY**, so as to make a firm, pliable, non-sticky dough.

2 Knead until smooth, about 5 min.

3 Roll dough, on floured board, this thin:

4 Cut into 1¼″ squares

5 Drop them into boiling, salted water

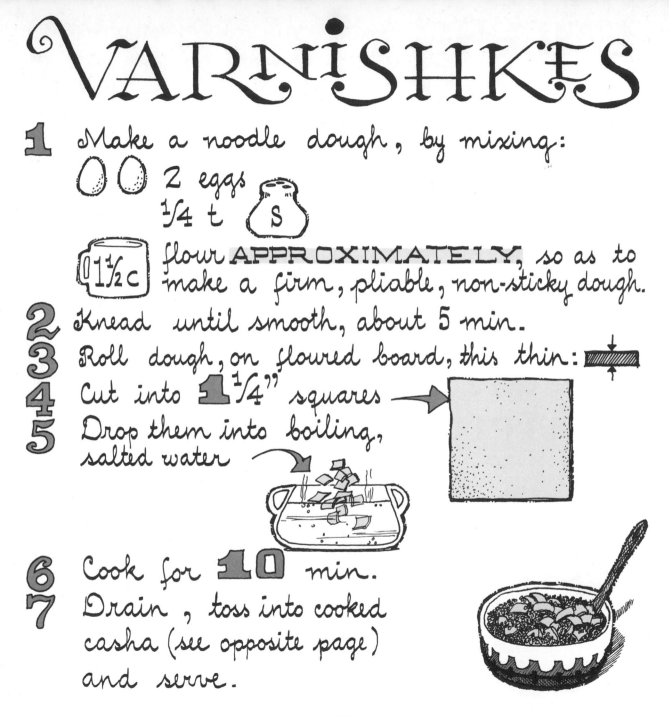

6 Cook for 10 min.

7 Drain, toss into cooked casha (see opposite page) and serve.

casha

1 c medium density buckwheat groats

1 egg

1 t S

1 T oil

2 c boiling water

2 T fried onions (p.40) ➡ you may substitute crisp bacon bits or grieven (p.84)

1 T shmaltz or margarine

1/4 t P

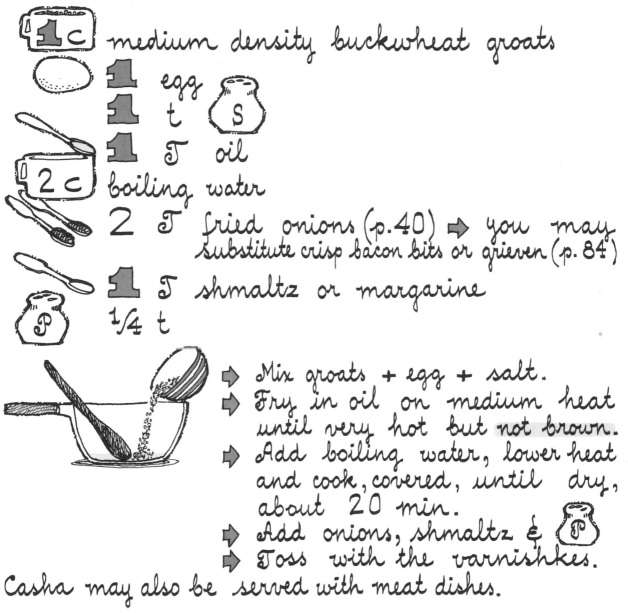

➡ Mix groats + egg + salt.
➡ Fry in oil on medium heat until very hot but not brown.
➡ Add boiling water, lower heat and cook, covered, until dry, about 20 min.
➡ Add onions, shmaltz & P
➡ Toss with the varnishkes.

Casha may also be served with meat dishes.

varenikes

➡️ Make a noodle dough, by mixing:

2 eggs

¼ t

1½ C flour, APPROXIMATELY, so as to make a firm, pliable, non-sticky dough.

➡️ Knead smooth & on floured board roll this thin: ➡️ 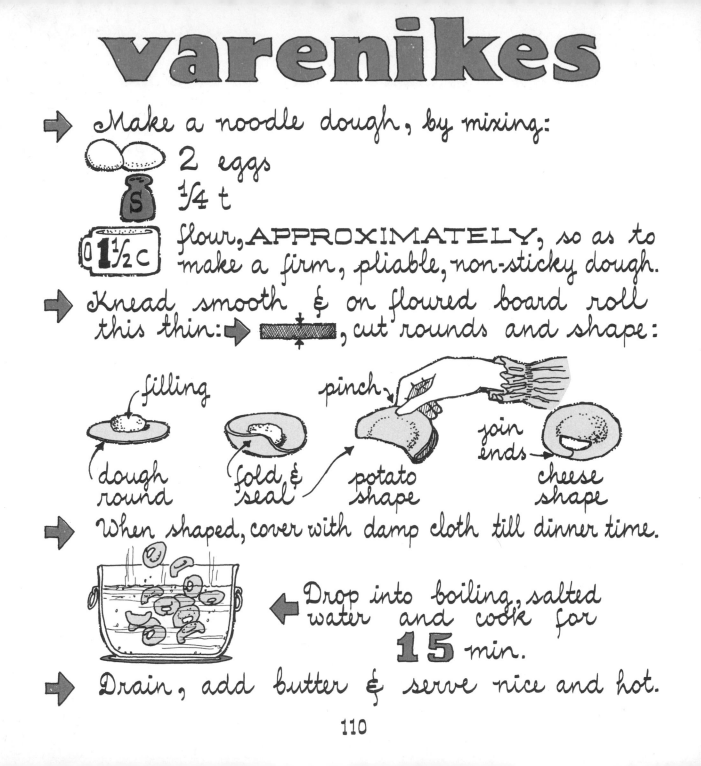, cut rounds and shape:

filling   pinch

dough round   fold & seal   potato shape   join ends   cheese shape

➡️ When shaped, cover with damp cloth till dinner time.

⬅️ Drop into boiling, salted water and cook for **15** min.

➡️ Drain, add butter & serve nice and hot.

fillings for varenikes

POTATO FILLING

Mix:

1 potato, boiled in jacket, peeled and mashed

S

P

1 T fried onions see p. 40

CHEESE FILLING

Mix:

1 pt. baker's or farmer's cheese, passed through sieve

¼ t S

1 egg

1 T SUGAR

FAREEL

➡ Knead until smooth:

2 eggs + ¼ t S and

1½c flour, MORE OR LESS ➡ to make a firm, but not crumbly, dough.

➡ Roll on floured board.
➡ Let rest to dry but not harden.
➡ Cut in long strips, then mince.

➡ Spread minced noodles out & let dry some more. (If you let them dry thoroughly, you can store for future use.)
➡ Cook in boiling, salted water 10 min. ➡ drain & serve.

Variations on the theme

A. Macaroni: ➡ leave dough in long strips.
B. Spinach noodles: ➡ to the dough, add spinach leaves mashed to a pulp & strained ➡ add more flour as needed.
C. Humble noodles: ➡ replace 1 egg with 5 T water.
D. Miserly noodles: ➡ skip the eggs altogether and make the dough out of water, flour and salt.

Buckwheat Berlej

→ Knead until smooth.

2 c buckwheat flour

1 egg + **¼ t** **S**

cold water, added by drops, almost, so as to make a firm, but not crumbly, dough.

→ Roll into ¼" fingers.

→ Cut into 3⁄4" lengths.

drop in

boiling, salted water

→ Cook until the berlej float, about 5 min. drain & serve

serving suggestions on p. 102.

Peisaj'ke Lockshen
Passover noodles

For each [egg] → measure water in 2 half shells → 1 T potato starch → pinch salt

> Corn starch or flour will do almost as well

A Dissolve starch in the measured water.

B Mix with eggs and salt.

C Fry very thin pancakes, turn only once lightly greased pan on medium-high heat

D when golden roll up and cut into thin strips.

✳——✳——✳

Dump lockshen into hot broth 1 min. before serving. Or better yet, serve them in a bowl and let people dump their own.

EMPANADAS

The empanada is the south American knish. There are baked empanadas and deep-fried empanadas.

FILLING FOR EMPANADAS

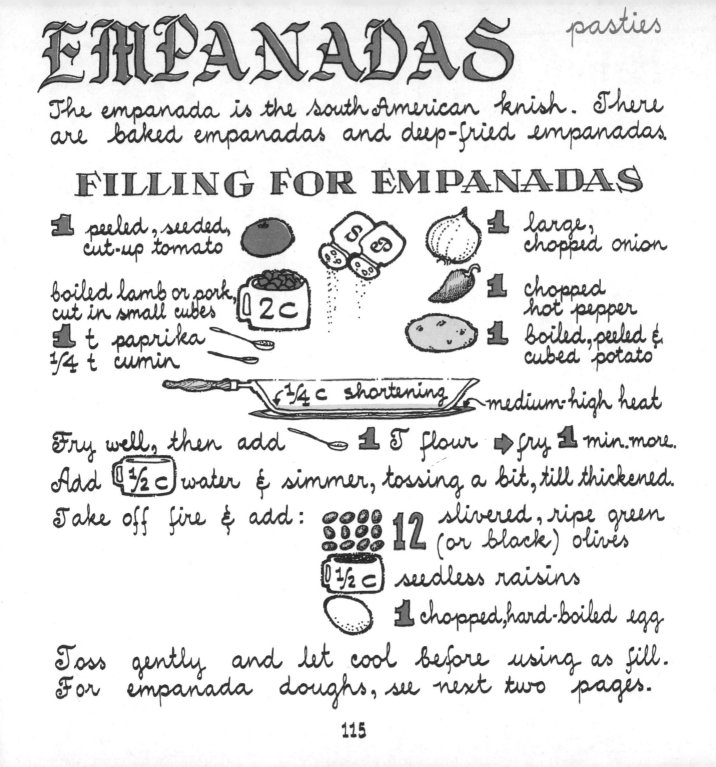

1 peeled, seeded, cut-up tomato

1 large, chopped onion

boiled lamb or pork, cut in small cubes

1 chopped hot pepper

1 t paprika
¼ t cumin

1 boiled, peeled & cubed potato

¼ c shortening — medium-high heat

Fry well, then add **1** T flour ➡ fry **1** min. more.

Add ½ c water & simmer, tossing a bit, till thickened.

Take off fire & add:

12 slivered, ripe green (or black) olives

½ c seedless raisins

1 chopped, hard-boiled egg

Toss gently and let cool before using as fill. For empanada doughs, see next two pages.

baked EMPANADAS

½ t S

¾ C water, approximately, for rather firm dough

⅓ c shortening

3 c flour

Mix and knead until smooth.

➡ see p. 115 for filling ⬅

1 make 1½" balls

2 roll them thin

3 fill them

4 dampen edges, slightly

5 pinch sealed

6 flute edge

7 brush tops with beaten egg white for gloss

8 bake at 400°F for 25 min. or until light brown.

fried EMPANADAS

½ t S   1 c water, approximately, for medium firm dough

¼ lb. soft margarine   3 c flour

Mix ➡ let rest 15 min. ➡ knead until smooth
➡ see p. 115 for filling ⬅

1 on floured board, roll into a large rectangle

2 grease thinly, with soft margarine & sprinkle with flour

3 fold over

4 repeat #2

5 fold again

6 roll about ⅛" thick

7 cut dough rounds

8 fill; and dampen edge

9 seal gently

10 drop in

WARM OIL

11 When layers begin to open, increase fire to very hot, turn empanadas once ➡ cook till brown ➡ drain & serve.

knishes

Knishes are little morsels made of dough, stuffed with goodies and baked. They serve all kinds of purposes; there are knishes for main courses, knishes for side dishes, knishes for lunches and parties and picnics and naturally knishes for nashers.

some doughs for knishes

1. Israel dough   (p. 120) ➡ Any filling
2. Humentashen dough (p. 152) ➡ Cheese filling
3. Strudel dough   (p. 156) ➡ Any filling

some fillings for knishes

1. Casha   ⬅ (p. 121)
2. Cheese   ⬅ (p. 122)
3. Liver & potato   ⬅ (p. 122)
4. Potato   ⬅ (p. 123)
5. Ground beef & potato ⬅ (p. 123)

how to shape a knish with Israel or humentashen dough

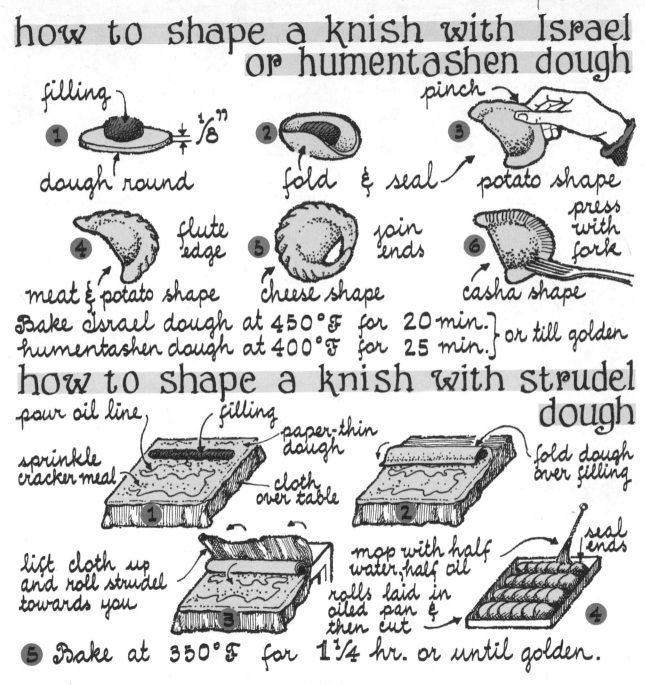

filling → ① dough round ‡ 1/8"

filling

② fold & seal

pinch ③ potato shape

④ flute edge — meat & potato shape

⑤ join ends — cheese shape

⑥ press with fork — casha shape

Bake Israel dough at 450°F for 20 min.
humentashen dough at 400°F for 25 min. } or till golden

how to shape a knish with strudel dough

pour oil line / **filling**

sprinkle cracker meal

paper-thin dough

cloth over table

①

fold dough over filling

②

lift cloth up and roll strudel towards you

③

mop with half water, half oil

rolls laid in oiled pan & then cut

seal ends

④

⑤ Bake at 350°F for 1¾ hr. or until golden.

Israel Dough

A. Mix thoroughly:

3 c flour   boiling water   pinch baking soda

B. Add and mix until smooth and even: ½ lb. margarine.

C. Make 2 equal round patties

D. ➤ REFRIGERATE OVERNIGHT

NEXT DAY

E. On floured board, roll each patty this thin

F. With floured rim of a glass, cut circles.

G. Fill with any knish filling.

H. Shape as shown on p.119.

I Bake 450°F 20 min or until golden.

P.S. This dough can also be used for pie crusts. The remnants, sprinkled with coarse salt before baking, make fine crackers ⬅ Bake crackers 10 min. only.

Fillings for Knishes
pasties

CASHA FILLING

Put in a pot on medium heat:

1 T cooking oil

1 c dark buckwheat groats, medium density (there are 3 densities)

1 egg ➡ mix well with the buckwheat

S **1** t

Toast until very hot but NOT BROWN ⬅

Take pot off burner & add:

2 c boiling water

Put back on burner, cover, turn fire to LOW & simmer till dry, about 20 min.

off fire mix in: ➡

2 T fried onions (see p.40)

1 T shmaltz or margarine

P ¼ t

➡ Taste & adjust the **S**

CHEESE FILLING

Mix :

1 pt. baker's or farmer's cheese, passed through a sieve

1 egg ➡ mixed not beaten

2 T sugar

3/8 t & PINCH ➡

1/4 c raisins ⬅ optional

1/2 t cinnamon ⬅ optional

see p.118 for doughs for knishes.

LIVER & POTATO FILLING

Fry evenly: **1/4** lb. cut-up chicken livers

in: **1** T shmaltz or margarine

grind or mash well then add:

1 large cooked, peeled and mashed potato

1 T fried onion (see p.40)

122

POTATO FILLING

Mix :

1 large cooked, peeled, mashed potato

1 T fried onion (see p. 40)

1 t shmaltz or margarine   S & P

Some grieven if you have any.

GROUND BEEF & POTATO FILLING

Fry : **1** lb. crumbled, lean ground beef, in
1 t margarine

Toss until all pink is gone ➡ remove from fire.

Mix with : 2 large cooked, peeled and mashed potatoes

2 T fried onion (see p. 40)

1 t sugar

For a Peruvian tang fry the meat with:
cut up & seeded tomato + hot pepper + green pepper

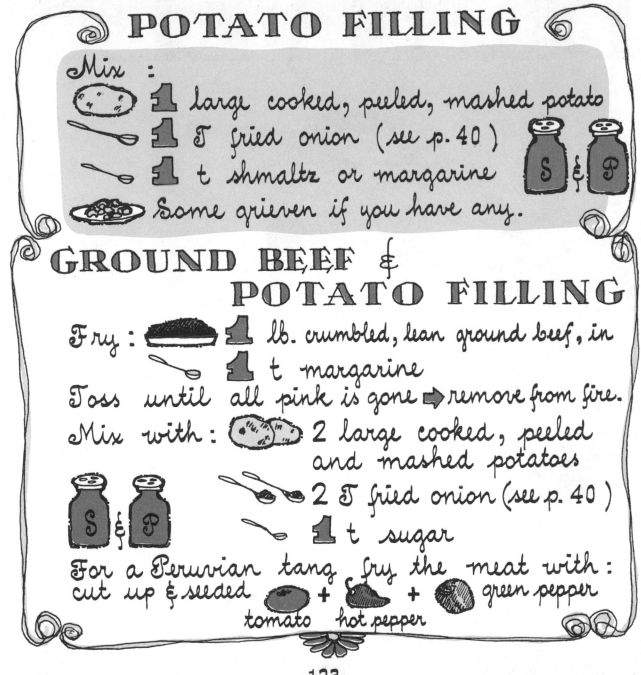

BLINTZES

filling

1 pt. baker's or farmer's cheese passed through sieve →

SUGAR 2 T and 3/8 t **S**

1/8 t white pepper

2 beaten eggs ➡ add only as much as will make a mixture that holds its shape.

wrapping

Beat : 2 egg yolks
1¼ c milk
¼ t S

Add : 1 c flour & mix to a smooth batter.

1 on barely oiled pan, fry large, thin pancakes, on one side only

2 drop on cloth

3 fried side up, fold on dotted lines to wrap a neat pack

gob filling

4

set folded side down on greased baking sheet

5 bake at 350°F for 20 min. or till tops are brown.

➡ serve hot blintzes with sour cream & jam ⬅

125

Salty Noodle Kugel

1 ½ lb. noodles ➡ boil in salted water for **10** min. ➡ rinse & drain well.

2 4 large eggs ➡ mix into noodles + S & P

3 In a pudding pan, heat up ½ c cooking oil or shmaltz ➡

4 Pour most of the hot oil into the noodle mixture and blend ➡

5 Now pour noodle mixture into the hot, oiled pudding pan & cover ➡

6 Bake in preheated 400°F oven for **1** hr. then uncover & keep baking till top is brown.

Sweet Noodle Kugel

Do as for salty except as follows:

➡ Use oil ➡ never shmaltz

➡ Omit the P

➡ Add: ¼ c orange juice and ¼ t grated orange rind

➡ Mix in fruit slices such as apple or banana & lots of raisins.

Matzo meal Bocaditos

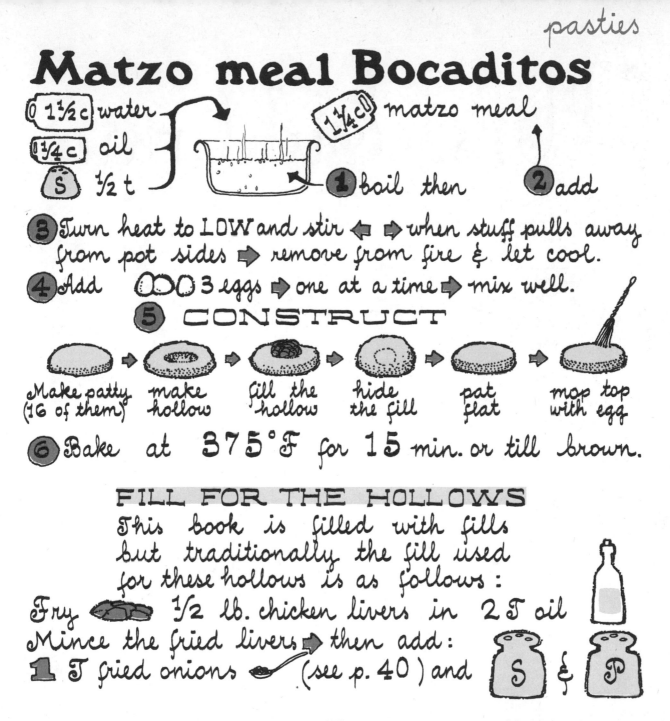

0 1½c water
1/4 c oil
S ½ t

1/4 c matzo meal

1 boil then **2** add

3 Turn heat to LOW and stir ⬅ ➡ when stuff pulls away from pot sides ➡ remove from fire & let cool.

4 Add ⬯⬯⬯ 3 eggs ➡ one at a time ➡ mix well.

5 CONSTRUCT

Make patty (16 of them) ➡ make hollow ➡ fill the hollow ➡ hide the fill ➡ pat flat ➡ mop top with egg

6 Bake at 375°F for 15 min. or till brown.

FILL FOR THE HOLLOWS

This book is filled with fills but traditionally the fill used for these hollows is as follows :

Fry ½ lb. chicken livers in 2 T oil

Mince the fried livers ➡ then add:

1 T fried onions (see p. 40) and **S** & **P**

127

Mrs. Eidelman's

tube pan

1/2 c — BROWN SUGAR

2 eggs

4 egg yolks

13 oz. — sweet condensed milk

13 oz. — evaporated milk

1/8 t & 1 t vanilla — S

water in flat pan

wood spoon

mixing bowl

toothpick

Flan

1. Put tube pan, with sugar in it, on medium heat & with wood spoon, spread the melting sugar all over the inside ➡ set aside. ➡
2. In bowl mix the eggs & yolks ➡ do not beat.
3. Mix in the milks, salt & vanilla.
4. Pour the mixture into the sugar coated pan.

1" water inside flat pan

5. Place tube pan on flat pan in 450°F oven & bake for 20 min. ➡ Test with toothpick; if it comes out clean, it's done.
6. Let flan cool ➡ loosen edges with point of a knife ➡ put plate on top & turn upside down.

Budín de Arroz

es Rice pudding so

A 1 Qt. milk
1 C white rice — soak for 45 min.

B Put ↑ on LOW fire and cook covered until rice is tender. — about 45 min.

C Put ↑ into and add:

blender
blend at high speed

SUGAR 3/4 C
2 eggs
3 egg yolks
1/4 t ground orange rind
S 1 t
1 t vanilla

D Peruvians like to add 1/2 c raisins after blending.

E Pour rice mixture into pudding pan previously buttered & dusted with powdered sugar.

outer pan with 1" water

F Bake in 350°F oven 1 1/4 hr. test center with a toothpick if clean ➡ it is done.

Serve warm or chilled.

serves 10

Arroz con Leche

∽ Rice with milk ⌇

A cover

1 Qt. milk
½ c white rice

soak overnight in refrigerator

B Put on medium heat until hot but not boiling, cover & cook until rice & milk form a thick mass ➡ stir once in a while.

about 1 hr.

C Add:

SUGAR ½ c

S ½ t

½ t vanilla

Cook 1 min. more

D Pour into individual bowls & CHILL.

cinnamon   nutmeg

E Sprinkle just before serving.

serves 6

budín de manzanas

∾ Apple pudding ∾

3 eggs ⇨ separated   &   oil ¼ c

1 t vanilla   &   S ⅜ t

¾ c cream of wheat

2 lb. green apples

SUGAR ½ c (add more if apples are sour)

1 Mix: yolks + oil + vanilla + salt + cream of wheat.

2 Coarsely grate the peeled apples (discard core) into cold, salted water ⇨ squeeze dry and add to yolk mixture.

3 Beat whites, adding sugar, till soft peaks form; ⇨ fold into apple - yolk mixture.

4 greased pan 8" x 8" x 2" will do ⇨ Bake at 350°F about 35 min or until brown; ⇨ test with a toothpick ⇨ if clean, it's done.

no cream
PAPAYA ice cream

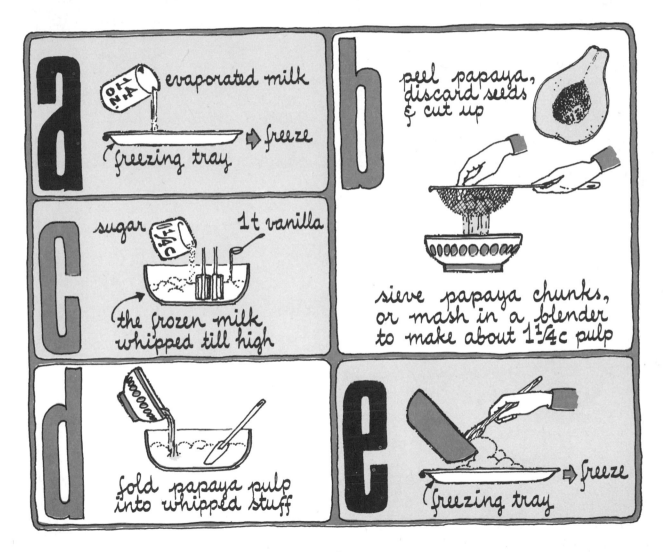

a evaporated milk — freezing tray ⇨ freeze

b peel papaya, discard seeds & cut up

sieve papaya chunks, or mash in a blender to make about 1¼c pulp

c sugar ¹⁄4c — 1t vanilla — the frozen milk whipped till high

d fold papaya pulp into whipped stuff

e freezing tray ⇨ freeze

NIDOS (nests)

1/4 lb. soft butter

2 heaping T sugar

2 eggs ▶ separated ▶ yolks   whites

1/2 t vanilla or (1/4 t lime juice &)
1/8 t (1/4 t grated rind)

1 c flour   STRAW ◀ fruit preserves & walnut meats

▶ Beat butter & sugar until fluffy.
▶ Beat in egg yolks, one at a time.
▶ Beat in vanilla (or lime) and salt.
▶ Mix in flour ▶ with a wood spoon ▶
▶ Make 1" round balls o o o . o ... o . . . . . .
▶ Dip each ball in

egg whites   ball,   poke   fruit   pieces
               hole   preserves   walnut
buttered & floured cookie sheet

◀ TOP VIEW
3 pieces walnut   ▶ Bake ▶ 400°F 15 min.
stuck on rim
fruit preserves   or till light gold.

134

RUSSIAN sugar cookies

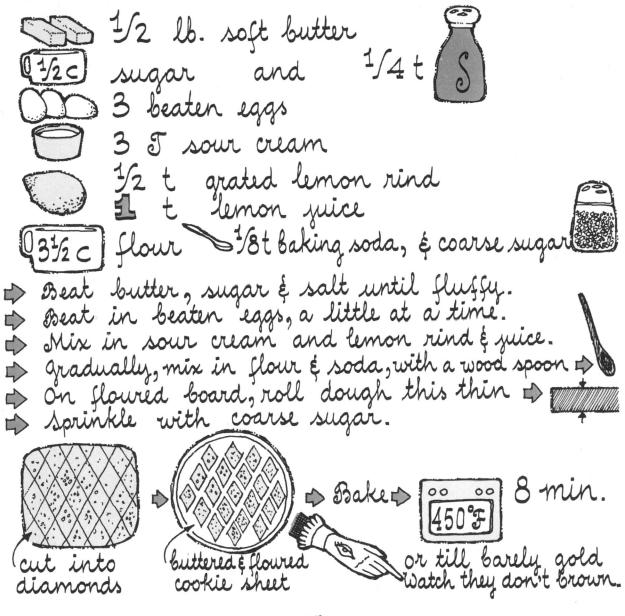

½ lb. soft butter

½ c sugar and ¼ t S

3 beaten eggs

3 T sour cream

½ t grated lemon rind

1 t lemon juice

3½ c flour ⅛t baking soda, & coarse sugar

➭ Beat butter, sugar & salt until fluffy.
➭ Beat in beaten eggs, a little at a time.
➭ Mix in sour cream and lemon rind & juice.
➭ Gradually, mix in flour & soda, with a wood spoon ➭
➭ On floured board, roll dough this thin ➭
➭ Sprinkle with coarse sugar.

cut into diamonds

buttered & floured cookie sheet

➭ Bake ➭ 450°F 8 min.

or till barely gold. Watch they don't brown.

rugged Russian cookies

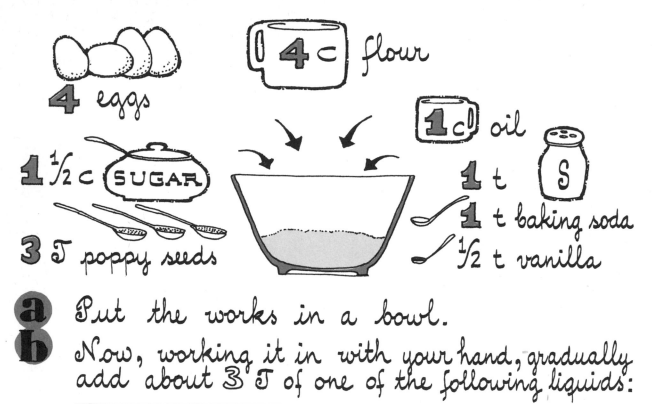

4 eggs

4 c flour

1 c oil

1½ c SUGAR

3 T poppy seeds

1 t S

1 t baking soda

½ t vanilla

a Put the works in a bowl.

b Now, working it in with your hand, gradually add about 3 T of one of the following liquids:

CHOICE OF LIQUID:

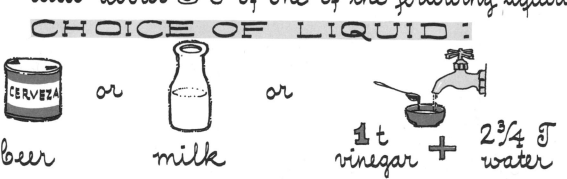

CERVEZA   or   or

beer   milk   1 t   +   2¾ T
                          vinegar   water

c stop adding the liquid when the dough is hard but not crumbly; and when touched with clean finger, it's not sticky.

IF TOO WET OR STICKY: ADD FLOUR.

d On a floured board, roll this thick:

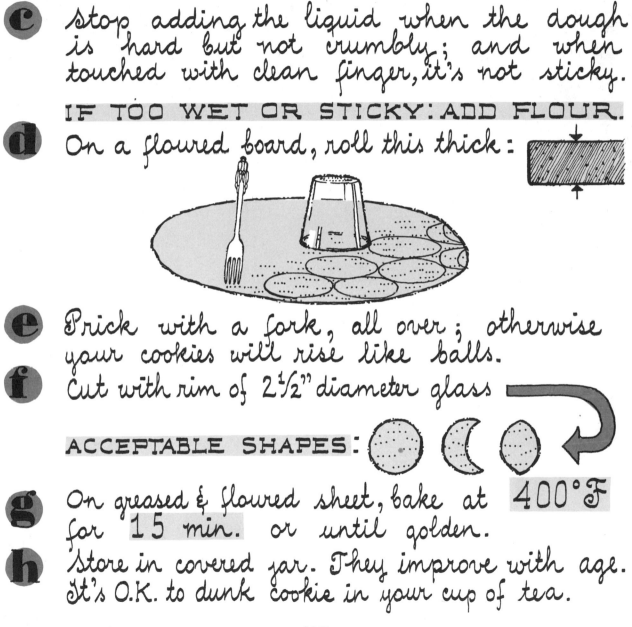

e Prick with a fork, all over; otherwise your cookies will rise like balls.

f Cut with rim of 2½" diameter glass

ACCEPTABLE SHAPES:

g On greased & floured sheet, bake at 400°F for 15 min. or until golden.

h Store in covered jar. They improve with age. It's O.K. to dunk cookie in your cup of tea.

Alfajores ALBERTO

* ⅓ lb. margarine → beat until fluffy.
* ¾ c sugar & ¼ t S → beat in.
* 3 beaten eggs → beat in gradually.

✽ MIX:
* 1 t pisco or cognac
* ¼ t grated lemon rind
* juice of ½ lemon
* ½ t vanilla

✽ MIX-SIFT:
* 1½ c cornstarch
* 1 c flour
* ½ t baking powder

✽ ALTERNATELY MIX IN:

wet mixture → margarine mixture
dry, sifted mixture ←
wood spoon

* Mix till smooth → let rest 30 min.
* On board, dusted with cornstarch, roll dough this thin:
* With floured rim of small glass, cut rounds; then gently transfer them to a clean baking sheet, and bake at 325°F for 20 min. or until pale gold.
* Cool and fill between each pair of rounds with manjar blanco. If you wish, dust with powdered sugar.

Manjar Blanco Gringo cookies

← Keep boiling water level above can.

unopened can of sweet condensed milk
(shake well & remove label beforehand)

14 oz.

Boil **1½ hr.** ➡ Cool ➡ Open ➡ Use

Manjar Blanco the hard way

1 vanilla stick
or 2 t extract

⅔ C sugar
⅛ t baking soda

1 Qt. milk

Simmer, stirring frequently with a wood spoon, until milk starts to thicken, about **1½ hr.** then stir continually until done.

➡ test for done ⬅

a. color is a light gold

b. drop a spoonful into cold water ➡ it should harden to putty consistency

❀ Cool and use to stuff baked pastries, like alfajores.

Esther's cookies

¾ c soft margarine

1 c

1 egg

=3 c flour

3 T very hot water

½ t baking soda

¼ t

½ t vanilla

2 oz. melted, unsweetened baker's chocolate

1. Beat margarine with sugar until fluffy.
2. Beat in egg. Then, one at a time,
3. mix in: **1c** of the flour,
   the hot water,
   soda, salt & vanilla,
   the remaining **2c** flour.
4. Cut the dough in 2 halves ➡
5. Mix the melted chocolate with one of halves ➡
6. On wax paper, roll each half into ⅜" thick rectangle.
7. Flop one over the other & remove top wax paper.
8. Roll up by lifting one end of bottom wax paper.
9. Refrigerate for at least **1** hr. ➡ slice ¼" thick cookies & arrange on ungreased baking sheet **1** ½" apart.
10. Bake at 400°F for 12 min. or till light brown.

Palitos para té

Little sticks for tea

1 ¼ lb. margarine ➡ beat until fluffy.

2 ⅔ c powdered sugar & ¼ t S ➡ beat in gradually.

3 3 egg whites ➡ beat in a bit at a time.

4 Blend in:

¾ c flour

¼ c cornstarch

2 t vanilla

5 squeeze dough through decorator nozzle, making thin, longish sticks, onto buttered & floured baking sheet.

6 Bake at **425°F** for 5 min. or till edges begin to brown.

cachitos

∾ Little horns ∽

1 lb. crushed, blanched almonds (or Brazil nuts + bit almond flavoring). You can use blender to crush the nuts.

½ lb. powdered sugar

brush→

2 egg whites ⇒ set aside 2 t ⇒

1 T apricot jam

½ t vanilla

⅛ t and ¼ c crushed walnuts

a Mix all, except the **2** t whites & crushed walnuts.

b Working on a floured board make sculptures:

form balls ⇒ roll them ⇒ make horns ⇒ brush on whites ⇒ sprinkle walnuts

c Arrange on a buttered & floured baking sheet.

d Bake at **350°F** for **18** min. or till light brown.

Nut Torte

My mother used to enjoy saying "If it takes flour it is bread, not torte".

8 eggs → separated →

2 T melted butter

1 lime → juice and grated rind → green part only

1 t vanilla

2 T seedless, fruit jam

1 t

3/4 c

1 lb. ground walnuts (peeled weight) 4 1/2 c approximately

Note: if you want to be thrifty and you don't mind calling it bread, substitute: 0 1/2 c of the nuts with  1 T flour.

Beat yolks till light, add: butter, lime, vanilla, jam and salt.

Beat whites till fluffy, add: sugar, a little at a time; beat till stiff but not dry.

Fold mixtures together gently ➡ do not stir.

Fold in the walnuts.

Pour the works into buttered & floured pan. 9" round, 2" high will do.

Bake 350°F 45 min.

Test with toothpick if clean = done.

Turn oven off ➡ open door ➡ let torte cool in oven. cut in 2 layers & cream between cream top & all around ➡ frostings follow ➡

Coffee cream frosting is very good with this torte.

chocolate torte

a In a bowl  beat till light yellow:

8 egg yolks, then add:

¼c cocoa + ¼c boiling water ➡ made into a smooth paste ➡ then cooled

2 T melted butter

grated skin of **1** orange (no white part, it would make torte bitter)

the juice of the orange

JAM **1** T seedless, fruit jam

S ½ t

Mix well

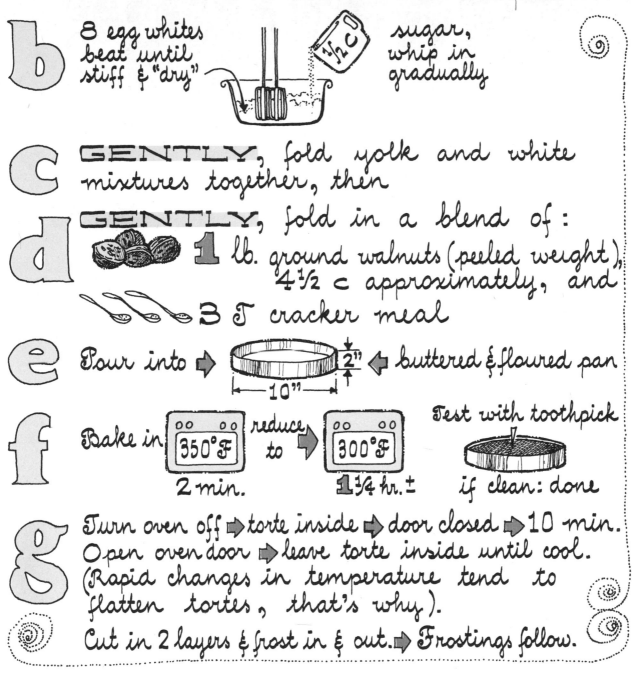

b 8 egg whites beat until stiff & "dry" — sugar, ½ c whip in gradually

c GENTLY, fold yolk and white mixtures together, then

d GENTLY, fold in a blend of: 1 lb. ground walnuts (peeled weight), 4½ c approximately, and 3 T cracker meal

e Pour into ➡ buttered & floured pan — 10" — 2"

f Bake in 350°F reduce to 300°F Test with toothpick
2 min. 1¾ hr. ± if clean: done

g Turn oven off ➡ torte inside ➡ door closed ➡ 10 min. Open oven door ➡ leave torte inside until cool. (Rapid changes in temperature tend to flatten tortes, that's why).
Cut in 2 layers & frost in & out. ➡ Frostings follow.

FROSTINGS

Jamaica chocolate cream

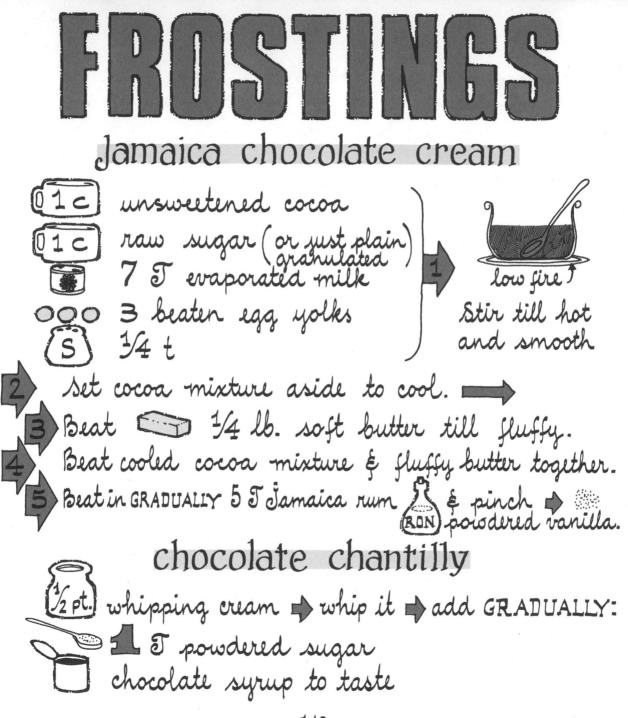

1 c unsweetened cocoa

1 c raw sugar (or just plain granulated)

7 T evaporated milk

3 beaten egg yolks

S ¼ t

1 → low fire ↑

Stir till hot and smooth

2 Set cocoa mixture aside to cool. ➡

3 Beat ¼ lb. soft butter till fluffy.

4 Beat cooled cocoa mixture & fluffy butter together.

5 Beat in GRADUALLY 5 T Jamaica rum & pinch powdered vanilla.

chocolate chantilly

½ pt. whipping cream ➡ whip it ➡ add GRADUALLY:

1 T powdered sugar

chocolate syrup to taste

coffee cream

½ lb. soft butter ➡ beat till fluffy ➡ add:
powdered sugar ⬅ GRADUALLY.
Now, add DROP BY DROP
2 t instant coffee dissolved in **1** t
hot water ➡ then cooled.

mocha frosting

½ lb. soft butter ➡ beat till fluffy ➡ add:
powdered sugar ⬅ GRADUALLY.
Then add, also GRADUALLY:

1 egg yolk

1 oz. melted, unsweetened baker's chocolate

1 t instant coffee mixed into the chocolate

½ t vanilla & ¼ t 🧂

Beat the works until smooth.

If after frosting the cake you wish to gild the lily,
ornament here and there with chantilly made of
whipped cream and a touch of powdered sugar & vanilla.

Cheesecake Raquel

1 ⟹ 2" 9"

Line greased pan with graham cracker crust (follow recipe on box)

2 ⟹ 13 oz. sweet condensed milk
7 oz. evaporated milk
6 egg yolks + 1 t S
1 lb. Ricotta cheese
grated rind and juice of 1 lemon

blend at high speed

blender

3 ⟹ 6 beaten egg whites — 1/2 C sugar, whip in gradually

4 Fold GENTLY **2** + **3** ⟹

5 Pour into ⟹ bake ⟹ 350°F 1¼ hr. approximately

6 Test with toothpick; if clean ⟹ turn oven off. Leave cake in oven with door open till cool ⟹ refrigerate.

APRICOT SOUFFLÉ

4 egg whites

(SUGAR) 3/8 c

½ lb. dried apricots ➡ minced and simmered with (1 C) water in covered pot 10 min. then cooled

(A.) Beat egg whites till soft peaks form ➡ gradually whip in sugar till high but not dry.

(B.) Fold the apricots into beaten whites, GENTLY.

(C.) Pour mixture into 2 equal, buttered pans (8"x8"x2"- O.K.).
➡ bake [325°F] about 20 min. ➡ till light brown

Let layers cool in pans, then ⬇ FILL between them.

FILLING:

oooo 4 beaten egg yolks

[14oz] evaporated milk

1 T cornstarch dissolved in a bit of the milk

(SUGAR) 3 T

½ t vanilla & ⅛ t [S]

double boiler

Cook, mixing continually, until thick.
Chill before filling between the layers of soufflé.

Hamentashen

1 SIFT ▶ cornstarch 1c 2c flour
sugar 1/2c S 3/4 t

2 ADD ▶ 1 T baking powder

3 SIFT THE WORKS ▶

4 BLEND TOGETHER ▶ pastry blender
3/4 c butter or margarine

5 ADD ▶ **3** well-beaten eggs

6 ROLL ▶ on a floured board ▶ this thick

7 SHAPE ▶
filling
cut circles   fill   fold up 3 sides   pinch seams tightly of 3-sided pyramid
brush top with beaten egg if gloss is desired

8 BAKE ▶ on ungreased pan 400°F for 12 min. or until light gold.

Filling for Humentashen

2 c prunes in water to cover

1 c poppy seeds in 1/2 c milk

1 SOAK OVERNIGHT IN REFRIGERATOR

2 NEXT DAY BLEND UNTIL SMOOTH:

the soaked prunes ➡ drained & pitted

the poppy seeds and milk

juice and grated rind of 1 orange

1/2 c sugar

blender

1/4 t ➡ nutmeg

1/4 t ➡ cinnamon

3 SIMMER UNTIL THICK ➡ about 20 min.

then ➡ COOL IT

To make poppy seed humentashen use 3 c poppy seeds in 1 c milk and 1/2 c prunes; the rest is the same.

Camishbroit

·~ Nut bread ·~

4 large eggs
(or 5 small ones)

2 c SUGAR

grated skin & juice of **1** lemon

3 c shelled walnuts ▷ rolled a bit but not crushed

¼c oil

½ t
¾ t baking soda
¼ t vanilla

5 c flour

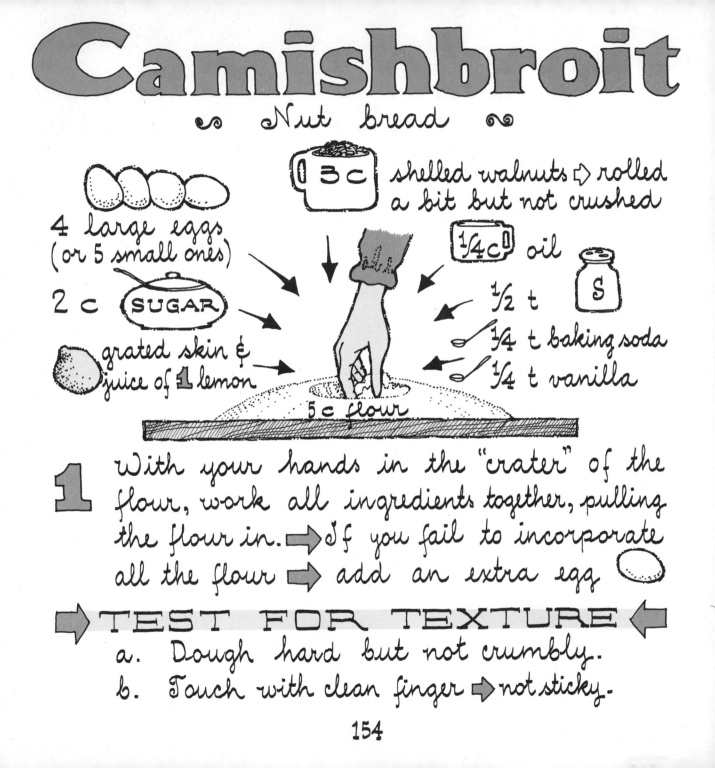

1 With your hands in the "crater" of the flour, work all ingredients together, pulling the flour in. ➡ If you fail to incorporate all the flour ➡ add an extra egg ◯

➡ TEST FOR TEXTURE ⬅

a. Dough hard but not crumbly.
b. Touch with clean finger ➡ not sticky.

2 SHAPE:
With oiled hands form the dough into 3 or 4 well-packed (no voids) flattened loaves.

brush tops with mixture of:
- **1** egg
- ½ t oil
- ½ t SUGAR

greased & floured baking sheet

3 BAKE ➡ 350°F *reduce to* ➡ 250°F *take out*

1 hr.   ¼ to ½ hr.

Tops should be golden and a toothpick inserted in the camishbroit should come out clean.

4 Cool to lukewarm ➡ cut into ½" slices ➡ when cold store in covered containers ➡ taste improves with age.

About camishbroit my mother used to say, "the less it grows during baking, the better".

strudel

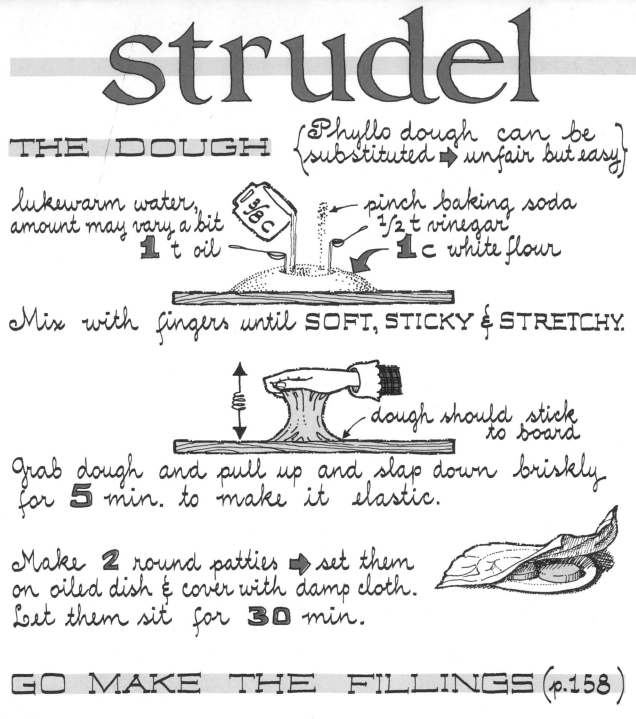

THE DOUGH

{Phyllo dough can be substituted ➡ unfair but easy}

lukewarm water, amount may vary a bit
1 t oil

pinch baking soda
½ t vinegar
1 c white flour

Mix with fingers until SOFT, STICKY & STRETCHY.

dough should stick to board

Grab dough and pull up and slap down briskly for **5** min. to make it elastic.

Make **2** round patties ➡ set them on oiled dish & cover with damp cloth. Let them sit for **30** min.

GO MAKE THE FILLINGS (p.158)

CONSTRUCTION DETAILS

➡ Cover a 2 foot-square table with a tablecloth &
➡ dust it with flour. ➡ With a rolling pin, roll each one of the patties into a 6-or 8-inch circle.
➡ Drape circle on floured hands and like an expert pizza maker enlarge circle and make it thin ➡
➡ By the time dough skin is covering your elbow (not mandatory) place it back on the table.
➡ Stretch edges around and around until paper thin dough goes over the edges of the table.
➡ Holes in the dough are frowned upon but not forbidden. ➡ Cut off thick edges all around.

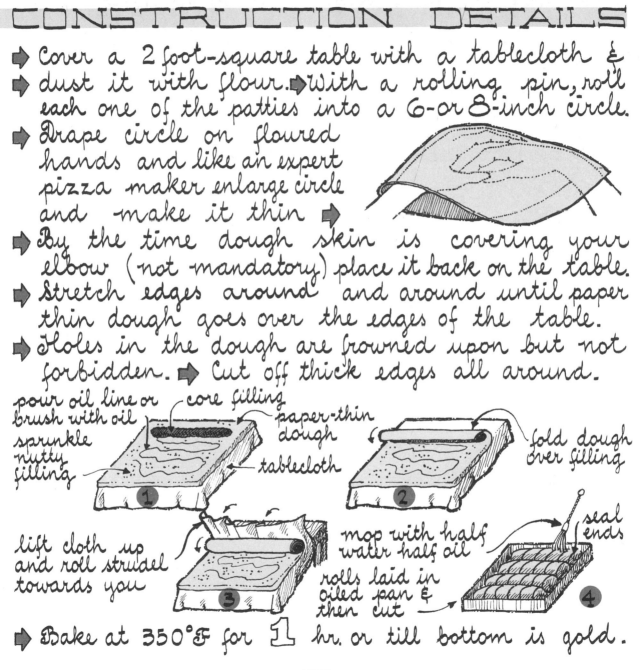

pour oil line or — core filling
brush with oil — paper-thin dough
sprinkle nutty filling — tablecloth
1

fold dough over filling
2

lift cloth up and roll strudel towards you
3

mop with half water half oil
rolls laid in oiled pan & then cut
seal ends
4

➡ Bake at 350°F for 1 hr. or till bottom is gold.

strudel fillings

FILLING FOR SPRINKLING

2c crushed, shelled walnuts

2c crumbled, stale, but not dry, bread

SUGAR **1** c

grated rind and juice of **1** lemon

1 T (heaping) seedless fruit jam

½ t cinnamon and ¼ t **S**

With fingers, mix all until damp throughout.

see p.156 for strudel dough

FILLING FOR CORE

drained canned cherries

or

fruit preserves

or

peeled, cooked, drained apple slices

or

other, sweet, non-runny stuff.

flud'n

Flud'n is a sort of Jewish baklava, and is made of the same materials as strudel, but varying from it in the construction details. You can make flud'n out of commercially sold, paper thin baklava dough, which goes by the name of phyllo or yufka. But to make it from scratch, follow strudel dough recipe on p.156, up to where you have it paper thin & draped over the table's edge.

let dough dry a bit (if homemade only)

with sharp knife cut in pieces to fit baking dish

pyrex is best

The 2 patties of dough should yield 18 layers.

brush top with water + oil and sprinkle with nutty filling

cut before baking

6 dough layers, brush each with melted butter or oil (18 layers total)

nutty filling (see opposite page)

2" deep buttered dish

Bake at 300°F for 1 ½ hr. or until golden.

smétene cake

∽ Sour cream cake ∾

1 Beat until fluffy:

½ lb. butter or margarine

2 Beat in: 1 c powdered sugar

1 egg

1 T white vinegar

¼ t S

3 Separately, sift together:

3 c flour &

1 t baking powder

4 Blend flour mixture into butter mixture.

5 Cut dough in 3 equal parts 1 2 3 .

6 On floured board, roll into 3 rectangles, 3/8" thick.

1   2   3

7 Bake in 350°F oven for 15 min. or until they start to brown ➡ Take out & let them cool.

8 MAKE THE FILLING:

Crush 1½ c walnut meats with a rolling pin

Mix with:
1 pt. sour cream
¾ c powdered sugar
S ¼ t

Separate ¼ of the filling mixture & combine it with ½ c thick apricot jam. Refrigerate both batches of filling, until firm enough to spread, about 1 hr.

9 CONSTRUCT THE CAKE:

apricot flavored filling
plain filling
top with plain filling
baked pastry layers

Refrigerate a few hours before serving.

KUCHEN

1 pastry blender
1 c flour
½ lb. butter
or margarine

Blend well and shape into a ball.
If too soft to handle, refrigerate for 1 hr.

2 ¾ t S
2 egg yolks
1 cake yeast, dissolved in ½ c warm milk
2 c flour
½ c sugar

Mix and shape into another ball.

3 floured board

Work the 2 balls of dough into each other, not too long and not too thoroughly.

4 Divide the mixed dough into 3 parts A+B A+B A+B and on a floured board shape each one, thus:

roll into ½" thick rectangle

spread on the **filling** →

roll up & seal ends, as best you can

→ Set each roll in an individual, greased & floured pan → let rise for 15 min. & bake at 350°F for 40 min. or till well browned.

5 **filling**

¾ c dried prunes in boiling water to cover

1 c poppy seeds in ½ c milk

SOAK OVERNIGHT IN REFRIGERATOR

Next day, mash drained, pitted prunes in blender. Then, MIX with: the poppy seeds and milk

2 T melted butter + ½ c SUGAR

1 t grated orange rind + ½ t S

½ c chopped walnut meats.

163

PICARONES

Picarones, light, puffy, Peruvian doughnuts, dipped in syrup, are by tradition the final touch to a sidewalk dinner of anticuchos and corn on the cob.

1 c water

2 T margarine

1 c flour

4 egg yolks

4 egg whites, beaten to soft peak stage

1 t baking powder

oil on medium-high heat when deep frying

corn syrup

brandy

wood spoon

salty water

powdered sugar

1 Bring to a boil :   2 T margarine

1 c water

2 Add & mix rapidly :   1 c   flour

3 Turn fire to low and keep stirring **5** min.; remove from fire and let it cool.

4 Mix in egg yolks, one at a time.

5 Mix in beaten egg whites.

LEAVE IT ALONE FOR 20 MIN.

6 Mix in the **1** t baking powder.

7 Dip hand in salty water ➡ grab a lump of dough ➡ poke finger to make hole and drop into hot oil. When brown on one side turn over with end of wood spoon.

dunk   touch

when brown, drain on paper

warm corn syrup with brandy to taste

powdered sugar

BLET'L con dulce

1 THE DOUGH

⅓ lb. butter or margarine

2 eggs

½ c + ¼ t SUGAR

1 T honey

1 t vanilla

3 c flour, approximately, so as to make a smooth but somewhat brittle dough

Mix all together and on wax paper roll 2 equal rectangles to fit your baking dish. An 8"×8"×2" pyrex is O.K. (the wax paper is to transfer dough into dish; peel it off and discard ⟼ don't bake it.)

2 THE GOODIES

3/4 lb. walnut meats crushed with a rolling pin + SUGAR ½ c

½ lb. chopped dry figs

strawberry jam ¼ c

1 beaten egg white + 1 T SUGAR

3 THE MAKING OF THE BLET'L

g prick all over with a fork

f top layer of dough

e dot strawberry jam over the figs

d chopped figs

c ½ of nut + sugar mixture

b bottom layer of dough

a oiled baking dish

Bake at 400°F until light brown, about 20 min. Remove from oven and reduce temperature to 350°F.

Add layer of remaining nut + sugar mixture, press it down gently and brush top with beaten egg white + sugar.

Return blet'l to 350°F oven and bake for another 30 minutes. Top should be brown.

Stuffed Puffs

A Bring to a furious boil:

- 0¾c water
- ¼c oil or margarine
- SUGAR 1½ T
- S ½ t

furiously boiling

B Now, dump in all at once:

- 1c matzo meal

C Stir for **1** min. ➡ remove from fire ➡ set aside to cool.

D Mix in **4** eggs (one at a time, until absorbed).

E Spoon batter onto a greased baking sheet, in roundish gobs, about 2" diameter ➡ set 2" apart.

bake ➡ 450°F 15 min. reduce to ➡ 250°F 15 min.

F When baked, open them with a sharp knife; and put back in the oven, till dry inside, about 5 min. 250°F

G Let cool; then fill with pastry custard or crema chantilly; see opposite page. ➡

pastry Custard

Mix:

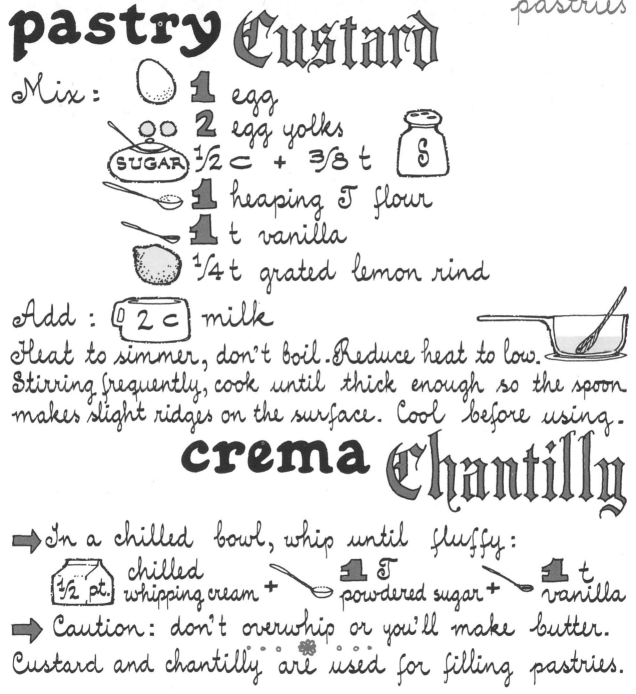

1 egg
2 egg yolks
½ c + ⅜ t [S]
1 heaping T flour
1 t vanilla
¼ t grated lemon rind

Add : [2 c] milk

Heat to simmer, don't boil. Reduce heat to low. Stirring frequently, cook until thick enough so the spoon makes slight ridges on the surface. Cool before using.

crema Chantilly

→ In a chilled bowl, whip until fluffy:

½ pt. chilled whipping cream + **1** T powdered sugar + **1** t vanilla

→ Caution: don't overwhip or you'll make butter.

Custard and chantilly are used for filling pastries.

pastel de
manzanas

∽ Apple cake ∾

1 Beat until fluffy :

1/4 lb.
soft butter + SUGAR 1/2 c + S 1/2 t

2 Add 🥚🥚🥚 3 beaten eggs ⇨ a little at a time, so it does not curdle; but if it curdles, go ahead anyway.

3 times:

3 Separately, sift together

1 c   1 t
flour   baking powder

4 Blend flour mixture into butter mixture.

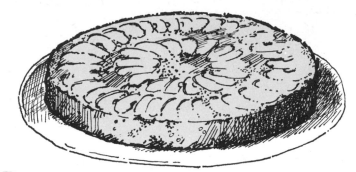

5 Peel, core & slice into cold, salted water

 4 apples ➡

6 Construct:

dust apples with 1/3 c powdered sugar

spoon flour-butter mixture on top **d**

dry the apple slices & arrange over paper **b**

a line bottom with wax paper

7 Bake at **375°F** for **30 min.**

8 Cool ➡ turn upside down ➡ remove paper.

Onik lakej

1 Beat as you go:

½ c   oil

SUGAR   1 c

4 eggs

1 c   honey

S   ¼ t

2 Mix dry ingredients:

flour   3 c

¼ t baking powder

¼ t cream of tartar

½ t baking soda

(for a nice dark color ↑)

3 Gradually add dry mixture to egg mixture and keep beating hard, to get plenty of air into the batter ➡

4 Blend in ¾ c broken walnut meats ➡ OPTIONAL

5 Bake in greased & floured pan, at ➡ 350°F reduce to ➡ 300°F   Test with toothpick

30 min.   45 min.   if clean: done

Mother used to say "When the honey cake is baking and the top cracks of its own accord, it's a good sign; it means it won't be gooey-heavy".

KOLACH

∽ Braided egg bread ∾

a Dissolve:
1 cake yeast

in **1** c warm water

b Mix: **3** T butter
SUGAR **3/4** c
3 beaten eggs
S **1¼** t
2 c warm water

c Mix:
a + b

d Gradually add
7½ c flour

e Drop the dough on extra **1** c flour and knead until quite elastic, about **10** min.

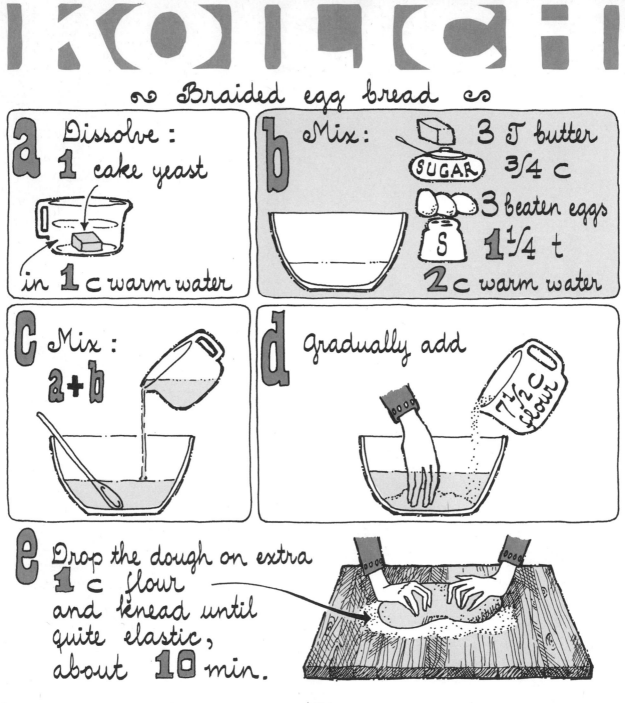

f Let dough rise, in a warm place, for 1 ½ hr. or till double in bulk, this way :

damp cloth
oiled bowl
oil top of dough

g knead again & divide into **4** parts ⬭⬭⬭⬭

and then, each part into **3** parts ⬭ ⬭ ⬭ &

roll them into long fingers

h Make chubby braids

i Set braids **4"** apart on greased & floured baking sheet; cover with a damp cloth and let them rise **30** min. or till double in bulk.

j Brush tops with beaten egg ⬭ & if you wish, sprinkle some sesame or poppy seeds; then

bake at **350°F** for **30** min. or till rich brown.

Bublichki or Rosquitas
Pretzels

2 c flour
2 T sugar
4 medium eggs
1 t S

1 Work into hard dough (like for noodles).

2 $3 \times 16 = 48$

Cut into 3 parts and each part into 16 parts.

3 Roll each part into a 6" finger, then join ends firmly.

4 Drop in, a few at a time — big pot, half full of __boiling__ water, the juice of ½ lemon & 2 T sugar

5 Cook for 2 or 3 min. → take out onto a towel.

Bake on ungreased baking sheet at 400°F → 20 min.

6 SHAPE ALTERNATIVES → knot   figure eight   serpent coil   peaceful pretzel

Peisaj'ke Bagel

Passover Bagels

1 Bring to a boil:
- 3/4 c water
- 1/4 c shmaltz or oil
- SUGAR 1½ T
- S ½ t

2 Dump in all at once:
- 1 c matzo meal

furiously boiling

3 Stir for **1** min. ➡ remove from fire ➡ set aside to cool.

4 Mix in **3** eggs (one at a time until absorbed).

5 With oily hands make **2"** balls ○ ○ ○ ...

set balls 1½" apart on greased baking sheet

poke hole with oily finger and spin in tight little circles, to widen the hole.

6 Bake: 450°F 18 min. reduce to 250°F 15 min.

Povet'l or prune jam

It would be difficult to remember a day when a jar of povet'l was not available at home. As a matter of fact, a thick, whole strawberry jam and povet'l, were pretty much the only ones we seemed to consume.

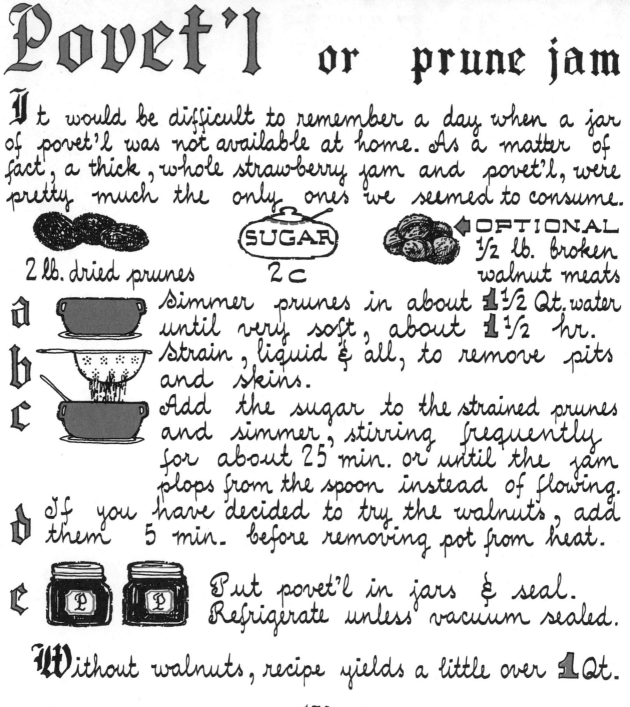

2 lb. dried prunes

SUGAR 2 c

◀ OPTIONAL ½ lb. broken walnut meats

a Simmer prunes in about 1½ Qt. water until very soft, about 1½ hr.

b Strain, liquid & all, to remove pits and skins.

c Add the sugar to the strained prunes and simmer, stirring frequently for about 25 min. or until the jam plops from the spoon instead of flowing.

d If you have decided to try the walnuts, add them 5 min. before removing pot from heat.

e Put povet'l in jars & seal. Refrigerate unless vacuum sealed.

Without walnuts, recipe yields a little over 1 Qt.

TIPS

To peel tomatoes, first dip them in boiling water for a minute. To remove seeds, cut in half and squeeze.

For making broth with bones or meat, simmer in water, then refrigerate until fat solidifies on the surface and is easily removed.

When chopping onions, or grating horseradish root, you may find that wearing snorkel glasses helps in maintaining one's equanimity.

If you are making mayonnaise, and it curdles, which means you may be adding the oil too rapidly, put a teaspoonful of cold water in a deep bowl and add the curdled stuff, a bit at a time, beating as you go.

If you are not a hot pepper eater, you can omit it from the recipes, or substitute a piece of any of the known sweet peppers.

When recipe calls for sliced fresh apples, plop peeled apples into cold, salted water until all sliced and ready to use. This will prevent their becoming brown. The same holds true for potatoes, but skip the salt.

Always preheat your oven before baking or roasting.

COOKERY
quackery

Warning: There is no guaranty that these home "remedies" will make you better, or for that matter, will not make you worse.

Regardless of their ethnic origin, these potions, poultices and hocus-pocuses were part and parcel of the kitchen lore. And to the effectiveness of several I can attest as a witness and, invariably reluctant, subject.

Bladder - To empty the bladder: boil corn silk, strain and drink the tea.

Boils - To open boils: make a bit of dough by mixing flour and water. Shape into a flat little disk, smear it with oil and place on boil. Cover with cloth or band-aid. Keep on for a day or so.

Cold - To relieve congestion from the common cold: string a few lemons & wear as a necklace.

Corns - To remove corns: place a slice of fresh tomato over the corn. Cover it with a cloth and leave it on overnight. When morning comes, the corn is supposed to be gone.

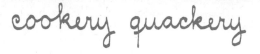

Ear - To soothe the earache caused by a cold: place two drops of warm (not hot) cooking oil in the ear. Follow with a sterile cotton plug.

Eye - To relieve simple eye irritation: apply over the closed lids, wads of sterile cotton, which have been previously dipped in a warm, strong tea solution. Repeat with fresh cotton wads as the ones on the lids get too cool.

Eyelashes - To grow long eyelashes (most effective when you are young): apply castor oil to the tips of the lashes once daily.

Facial - To cleanse and condition the skin of the face: spread egg yolk on entire face. Let it dry on the skin, without smiling or assuming any other change of expression, as this would cause wrinkles. Wash egg off face with soap and water. Rub an ice cube all over and pat dry.

Freckles - To remove freckles: rub the crushed skin of a chirimoya on the freckled areas. Leave on a few minutes; then rinse. Repeat daily. Chirimoya, commonly known as custard

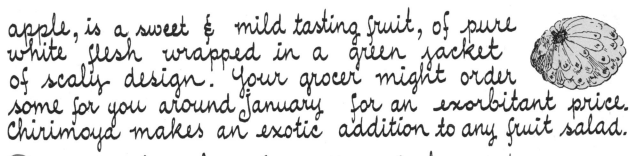

apple, is a sweet & mild tasting fruit, of pure white flesh wrapped in a green jacket of scaly design. Your grocer might order some for you around January for an exorbitant price. Chirimoya makes an exotic addition to any fruit salad.

Gas - For the relief of gas discomfort : put some orange peel in a bowl and add boiling water. Cover & let sit until water turns into a dark tea. Drink the tea hot.

Hands - For lovely hands: with a mixture of **1** T sugar and **1** T lemon juice, rub hands until they tingle. Rinse with cold water.

Headache - Place a slice of raw potato on each temple and hold them in place with a scarf or dish towel wrapped around the head. Replace with fresh slices of potato as they start to "wilt" and get warm.

Hiccups - Hold the breath while swallowing nine consecutive sips of water and keeping the eyes closed. Or eat a teaspoonful of dry sugar and follow by gently pressing the Adam's apple for a minute.

Indigestion - Drink warm tea made with camomile.

Insect stings - Apply to the afflicted area: iodized salt mixed with lemon juice. Or hold over it a clean cloth, soaked in vinegar, for about 15 minutes.

Menstrual cramps - To relieve cramps attributed to menstruation: drink hot tea made with oregano leaves, or tea made with cinnamon sticks.

Menstruation, delayed - To re-establish regularity of the menstrual period: drink hot tea made with parsley.

Onions - To remove onion smell from the hands: crush fresh parsley between hands and rinse; then rub with piece of lemon and rinse again.

Rheumatism - For the relief of rheumatic joint pains: beat **1** egg white until high. Add **1** t laundry soap flakes and continue beating until stiff. Spread the meringue on a cloth and apply over the aching joint. Leave on overnight, at least.

Sore throat - For the relief of sore throat due to a cold, there were several treatments, and they were administered either singly or consecutively, depending on the stamina and cooperation of the patient:

1 → gargle with ½ t [S] in [1 c] warm water.

2 Beat **1** egg yolk ○ adding [SUGAR] as you beat until you have a light yellow "gravelly" paste. Add a few drops of lemon juice → Swallow by spoonfuls without chewing.

3 Heat but do not boil:

[½ c] water

[½ c] milk

Add: ¼ t bicarbonate of soda.

→ Drink as much of it as you can stand and call it " okret mit milaj."

Glossary

ALFAJORES (Ahl fah ho′ress) Two cookie rounds filled with a thick milk and sugar cream called manjar blanco.

AMBREN (Ahm′brehn) Fried flour.

ANTICUCHOS (ahn tee coo′chos) Marinated beef heart barbecued on a skewer.

ARROZ (ah ros′) Rice.

ARROZ CON PATO (ah ros′ / kone / pah′toe) Rice and duck made in one pot.

BATIDO (bah tee′doe) Beaten or mashed.

BATIDO DE FREJOLES (bah tee′doe / day / freh ho′less) Literally meaning beaten beans, in Perú they are made by soaking beans until their skins are loose. Then the skins are patiently removed before the beans are mashed or strained.

BAYLICK FISH A kind of gefilte fish made with chicken breasts instead of fish.

BISTÉ (bees teh′) Steak.

BLET'L CON DULCE (bleh′t'l / kone / duel′say) Blet'l means page or sheet. Cookie dough sheets with sweet stuff in between.

BLINTZES (blinn′t'ses) A thin pancake filled with cheese.

BOCADITOS (bo kah dee′toes) Tidbits.

BUCKWHEAT BERLEJ (bear′leh) See page 102.

CABRITO (kah bree′toe) Young goat.

CARROT TZIMES (t'seh′mess) A sort of glazed carrot dish.

CASHA (kah′shah) Buckwheat groats.

CAUSA (cow′sah) Mashed cold potatoes with goodies on top.

CHARQUI (char′key) Jerky.

CHILCANO (cheel cah′no) A type of fish soup.

EMPANADAS (em pah nah′dahs) Pasties of meat filling wrapped in pastry dough—South American version.

FARFEL (far′fell) See page 102.

FLAN (flahn) The South American crème caramel or custard.

FLUD'N (flue′d'n) Pastry made of alternating layers of paper-thin dough and nut-sugar filling.

GEFILTE (gay fill′teh) Stuffed.

GRIEVEN (gree′vin) Chicken skin cracklings.

GUISO (ghee′so) Juicy pot stew. Literally, to prepare dishes by means of fire. In Perú guiso is used to describe dishes made by frying tomato and other stuff into a rich sauce in which the main item of the dish is ultimately cooked.

GUTIFARRAS (goo tee fah′rahs) Peruvian pork sandwiches.

HUMENTASHEN (who men tah′shen) Jewish pastry traditionally served during Purim. Made in a triangular shape and filled with prunes and poppy seeds, it is said to represent Haman's pockets.

HUMITAS (oo mee′tahs) Steamed grated corn in packets.

JUMUS (who moose′) Arab dish made of mashed garbanzo beans.

KNISHES (k'nish′ess) Pasties of varied filling wrapped in pastry dough—Jewish version.

KUGEL (coo′gull) A sort of noodle pudding.

KUJEN (coo´h'n) A poppy seed-filled coffee cake.

MALISNIK (mah liss´nick) A delicate cornmeal dish somewhere between corn bread and cormeal mush.

MANJAR BLANCO (mahn har´ / blahn´ko) A thick milk and sugar cream.

MATZO MEAL (mah´tzoh / meal) Commercially sold meal made of matzo, Jewish-type unleavened bread.

MATZO MEAL KNEIDLEJ (mah´tzoh / meal / k'nay´dlah) Matzo balls.

MECHADO (meh chah´doe) A type of marinated pot roast.

MENESTRÓN (meh nehs tron´) A thick soup made with meat and vegetables and flavored with pesto.

ÑOQUES (nyo´kess) See page 102.

OKOPA (o ko´pah) See page 38.

OKOPA AREQUIPEÑA (o ko´pah / ah ray key pay´nya) See page 38-39.

ONIK LAKEJ (oh´nick / lay´keh) Honey cake.

ONIONS, FRIED Jewish seasoning usually made in bulk.

PAELLA (pah eh´yah) A traditional dish of Spain made of rice, chicken, shellfish and so on all in one pot.

PAPAS (pah´pahs) Potatoes.

PAPAS A LA HUANCAINA (pah´pahs / ah / lah / wan kah yee´nah) A potato and cottage cheese salad.

PATO (pah´toe) Duck.

PELOTITAS (pay low tee´tahs) Little balls.

PEPIÁN (pay pyan´) Cooked grated corn.

PESTO (pehs´toe) A sauce used for flavoring made by crushing cheese and certain condiments in a mortar and pestle.

PICADILLO (pee kah dee´yo) Minced stuff. Dish made by frying together leftovers and other things.

PITA FALAFEL (pee´tah / fah lah´fell) Middle Eastern sandwich made with unleavened bread.

PLACHINTAS (plah cheen´tahs) A sort of Russian crêpe.

REFRITAS (ray free´tahs) Refried.

RELLENAS (ray yea´nahs) Stuffed.

SALSA (sahl´sah) Sauce.

SALTADO (sahl tah´doe) Tossed.

SHMALTZ (shmalts) Rendered poultry fat.

SMÉTENE (smeh´teh nay) Sour cream.

SOUR SALT Citric acid sold in Jewish delicatessens.

STRUDEL (shtrue´d'l) Pastry made with paper-thin dough, nuts and a rich filling, and rolled up.

TAMARINDO (tah mah reen´doe) Tamarind, see page 80.

VACA (vah´kah) Cow.

VARENIKES (vah reh´nee kess) See page 102.

VARNISHKES (var´nish kess) See page 102.

Index

About the author

Violeta Autumn's parents were part of a group of Russian Jews that immigrated to Peru, where they developed a cuisine combining the culinary traditions of both the Old World and the New. "My mother's cooking was so appreciated by the Jewish people living in Lima," Mrs. Autumn recalls, "that it was inevitable she would be talked into opening a sort of boarding house. It was my father's idea that all guests should have as many helpings as they wished. It was such a smashing success it closed up after only two months of operation."

Born in Chiclayo, Peru, Violeta Autumn studied architecture under Bruce Goff at the University of Oklahoma, graduating in 1953. After working for several architectural firms, she now carries on her own practice from her hillside studio-home in Sausalito, where she lives with her husband and son. In addition to designing buildings, Mrs. Autumn has worked as a delineator for other firms, executed several murals and even found time to paint, which led to exhibitions in the United States, Israel, Spain and Peru.

"I've always given my recipes in a graphic, have-fun way," Violeta Autumn states. "Friends were amused and delighted with them and suggested I ought to write a book that way." And thus she created "A Russian Jew Cooks in Peru," testing her mother's recipes, hand-lettering them and adding illustrations.